MITCHELL'S

THE STORY OF A STORNOWAY FAMILY'S GARAGE AND BUS BUSINESS

Colin Tucker.

MITCHELL'S

THE STORY OF A STORNOWAY FAMILY'S GARAGE AND BUS BUSINESS

COLIN TUCKER

Registered Charity SC047866

First published in 2018 by Acair, An Tosgan,
Seaforth Road, Stornoway, Isle of Lewis HS1 2SD

www.acairbooks.com

info@acairbooks.com

© text Colin Tucker 2018

© photos Mitchell family archives

The publishers are grateful to all individuals and organisations
who have supplied photographs and other material.

Map information supplied by Colin Tucker
and artwork created by Freya MacLeod 2018

The publishers are grateful for permission to reproduce photographs
and extracts from other materials. Wherever possible the copyright
holder has been acknowledged individually, but if it is brought to the
publisher's attention that anyone has been overlooked this will be
rectified in the next edition.

The right of Colin Tucker to be identified as the author of the
work has been asserted by him in accordance with the Copyright,
Designs & Patent Act 1988

Book and Cover design by David Caines.

A CIP catalogue record for this title is available from
the British Library

Printed and bound by Hussar Books, Poland

ISBN 978-1-78907-012-5

CONTENTS

Previous page: Typical of the buses owned by Mitchell's in the post-war years was this Bedford OB with body built by Duple, seen here on North Beach Street in Stornoway. It ran in the fleet from 1948 until 1964.

FOREWORD

Chris Mitchell

My grandfather John Mitchell established Mitchell's Garage and bus service in the 1920s and 30s, with the business passed down to my father Ian Mitchell when John passed away in 1961. My father then managed the garage until his retirement in 1995.

In 1981, aged 18 and while studying Business Law at the University of Glasgow, I learnt about the 1936 House of Lords court case, Mitchell vs the Stornoway Trustees, a contract law case concerning the rent of a triangular area of land in Stornoway. It was clear this case concerned my grandfather, and the location of Mitchell's Garage from the 1930s to the 90s.

I had not previously heard about the court case from my father. In fact, there were aspects of the case, and the impact of my grandfather's legal success, which were unknown to my father, who was born in 1933. My father was aware that animosities from some Trustees and others may have lingered for years following the court case, affecting aspects of the garage and bus service, but my grandfather didn't talk about that. My grandfather was described at such times as being thick-skinned and tenacious; he could talk straight to you, but there could be more behind his eyes that was left unsaid.

My father later reported that although he was committed to working in his father's garage, and had embarked on Vauxhall training for that purpose in the 1950s, when my grandfather suddenly died in 1961, my father was left 'holding the reins' of the garage business, for which he was ill-prepared at that time; his father hadn't shared much of the information needed to manage the operations of the garage and bus service.

I was born after my grandfather passed away, but enjoyed hearing about him and, from various anecdotes shared about him, pieced together an image of him as astute, wry and stoic. Once when collecting the fares from bus drivers at the end of their shifts, he confronted a driver who had been identified as pocketing some of the income for himself. When offered the day's takings by the driver, my grandfather declined them, saying that instead he'd prefer to have the money in the driver's pocket! On another occasion, my grandfather and father were at home for a meal when a report came in that there was a fire at the garage; instead of leaping up into action, as my father was doing, my grandfather continued eating, calmly saying that he'd head down to see what he could do, *after* his meal.

These and other stories from my father suggested that there might be interest in a book about Mitchell's Garage, which I encouraged my father to develop. Could such a book help provide a lens onto now-lost or forgotten aspects of the history, culture and lifestyles of the island at various points in the last century? My father was delighted that Colin Tucker agreed to research and write the book, but unfortunately, due to my father's passing in late 2016, he was unable to share more of his memories with Colin as the book developed. Nonetheless, there is much here uncovered by Colin which I didn't previously know, as well as many affirmations of what I did.

My father was always supportive of my interests and expressed no disappointment to me that I didn't plan to carry on the family business (and I feel sure he would have been equally supportive if I *had* been interested). Nonetheless, I was aware of some aspects of the garage which my father was happy to share with me. In the 1970s, he spoke of his struggles with the local Council over bus subsidies and his eventual decision to end the bus service. We also discussed the pros and cons of taking the roof off the car showroom in the 1980s, to save money on building rates.

I worked for a short time in the Parts Department, and occasionally with my mother Anne when she worked on the reception desk, where I was intrigued by the operation of the car hire business. I knew many of the staff: Ina and Chrissie in the office, and 'Tom', Norman and Kenny 'Keose' in other departments were all familiar and friendly. Staff loyalty always seemed to be high, and there was a sense of longevity and purpose to the business — many of the staff stayed with the garage for long periods.

I recall one car salesman was found to be defrauding the garage. The police were involved and the salesman may have been fined, but after the proceedings came to an end my father continued to employ the salesman. When asked why, my father responded that the man was an excellent salesman and a better one couldn't be found. Later on, the salesman was caught defrauding the garage again, and was once again kept on! My father charted his own course, no matter if it was sometimes unconventional.

When I was growing up, my father worked a lot, often six long days each week. He deliberated over the business in detail, liked to understand the procedural as well as psychological aspects of running a business, and took his time making strategic decisions. I didn't appreciate at the time the business pressures he might have faced, especially in the period following his own father's passing, and certainly not that there may have been related health concerns from those pressures. Indeed, my father tended to shield others from his problems. In the 1980s, he spent a few days in hospital in France following a car accident while on holiday by himself, but didn't tell anyone about this until he was released from hospital and back in the UK. (He was also at pains to make it clear that the accident was the fault of another driver!)

My father in later years did reflect on whether he should have spent more time with me when I was a child, and wondered if he'd spent too much time and energy focused on work. He was also concerned about having perpetuated his father's tendency to not share much. Thankfully, we did have many conversations over the years which evidenced my father's openness to sharing, and I was pleased that the idea for a book on Mitchell's Garage contributed further to those conversations between us. Together, my father and I visited the Stornoway Gazette office to look at 1930s editions of the newspaper, finding reports about the House of Lords court case and subsequent reports of Stornoway Trustees meetings, learning more about that history.

My father wrote a short speech to deliver at his 80th birthday party, and shared a draft with me beforehand for feedback. I was surprised to find that he referred to the event as a Mitchell's Garage employee reunion, and while there would indeed be many there who had worked in the garage and on the buses, many who had never worked at the garage had been invited to the party as well! Not wanting the event to be about himself and his birthday, he had instead deflected those ideas into the gathering being about the garage.

I am immensely grateful to Colin Tucker for writing this book, many others for their written and photographic contributions, all the staff at Acair for their interest and support in publishing this book, and David Caines for his excellent book design. We all hope the book meets our aspiration of providing a lens onto aspects of the island's life, culture and character which might otherwise be lost.

Christina MacLean and Catherine Anne Bain, the wives of John and Ian Mitchell, were crucial to the development of Mitchell's over the decades. I hope their positive impact will also be remembered.

INTRODUCTION

Colin Tucker

When I was asked by Ian Mitchell and his son Chris to write the story of the family and its businesses, I was both delighted and daunted. Delighted to be asked, and daunted when I discovered how little information there seemed to be. The sudden passing of Ian in December 2016 also meant that a vital source of much knowledge was gone.

Now after more than a little research and the help of a number of people who knew Ian or who worked for the Mitchells at one time or another, the story has been pieced together. It is a fascinating tale of family and business on the Isle of Lewis, a part of the island's history. To those of you who knew Mitchell's, I hope this will stir memories; for those of you to whom the story is new, I hope you can appreciate the part the family played in the social and economic history of the island.

I have tried to include a balance of bare facts and stories, of which there are many, more than could be included here. Both John and Ian were characters, as were many of their staff, and life seems never to have been dull. I have tried to ensure that there are no inaccuracies, but if there are any errors they are mine.

There are many people who must be thanked, for without their help I could not have completed the story. 'Tom' Maciver, Angus Macdonald, Mairi Mackenzie and Donald 'Dòmhnall Bhobsaidh' Macleod provided much knowledge and information. I would also like to thank those who provided photographs, including Ruairidh Murray, Lawrence MacDuff, John Sinclair and the Western Isles Transport Preservation Society. The staff of Stornoway Library must also be mentioned for their patience and help. To all these, and the many that I have not individually mentioned, I give my grateful thanks.

Chris was also a great help in keeping the writing on the correct track; for that thanks also. I hope the end product is a fitting tribute to his father and grandfather.

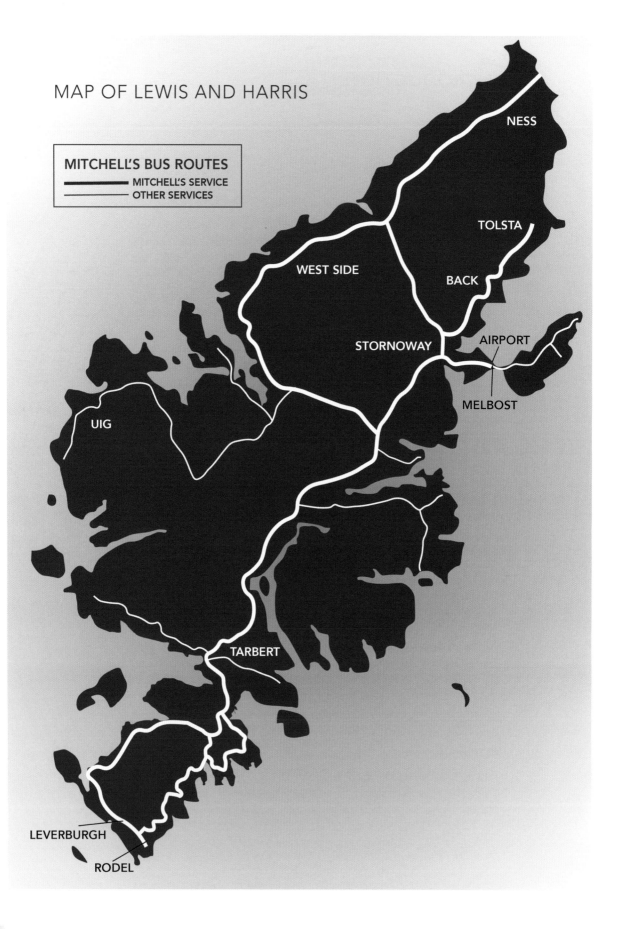

MAP OF LEWIS AND HARRIS

MITCHELL'S BUS ROUTES
——— MITCHELL'S SERVICE
——— OTHER SERVICES

NESS

TOLSTA

WEST SIDE

BACK

STORNOWAY

AIRPORT

UIG

MELBOST

TARBERT

LEVERBURGH

RODEL

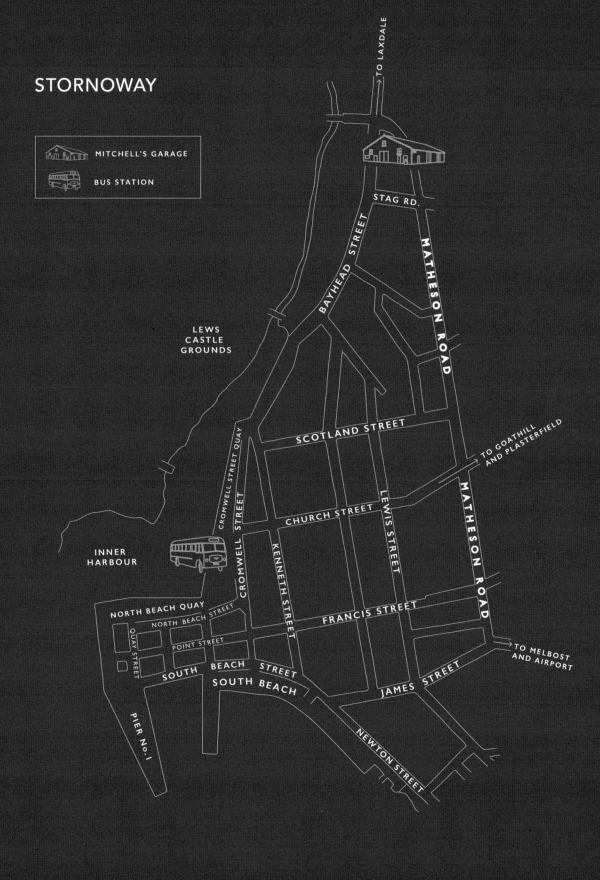

STORNOWAY

MITCHELL'S GARAGE

BUS STATION

TO LAXDALE

STAG RD.

BAYHEAD STREET

MATHESON ROAD

LEWS CASTLE GROUNDS

SCOTLAND STREET

TO GOATHILL AND PLASTERFIELD

CROMWELL STREET QUAY

CHURCH STREET

LEWIS STREET

CROMWELL STREET

MATHESON ROAD

INNER HARBOUR

KENNETH STREET

FRANCIS STREET

NORTH BEACH QUAY

NORTH BEACH STREET

POINT STREET

QUAY STREET

SOUTH BEACH STREET

SOUTH BEACH

JAMES STREET

TO MELBOST AND AIRPORT

PIER No. I

NEWTON STREET

1. JOHN MITCHELL

There is a photograph of John Mitchell taken during the First World War. In the uniform of a cavalry regiment he looks thoughtful, perhaps contemplating the horrors of war. He may be thinking back to happier childhood days on the croft, or it may be that he is considering his future. If it is the latter, then little will he know that it would be a future involving a major court case, owning and running a garage, and building up and operating a fleet of buses.

The year of eighteen ninety-two was not one of earth-shattering events; Queen Victoria was in the fifty-fifth year of her reign, while the British army was fighting a war in what was to become Nigeria. It was the year in which J R R Tolkien, Margaret Rutherford and Hugh MacDiarmid were born, while the death of Alfred, Lord Tennyson was recorded.

But an event which took place on 12 June 1892 was of greater importance to the inhabitants of South Shawbost, a small crofting township on the west side of the Isle of Lewis. Probably there was a great deal of anxious waiting, of pain and endurance, and an equally great deal of relief when a baby boy was safely born in the black house of number twenty-two. The baby was named John.

He was the son of George Mitchell, known locally as Seòras Dhòmhnaill Mitchell. George was a crofter, living at 22 South Shawbost. As well as working the croft George had made fishing his career. He was a man with a powerful physique and an affinity with the sea. He proved to be an excellent seaman and his services were sought after by skippers of East Coast fishing boats, which followed the herring down the east coast of Scotland and as far as East Anglia. The Mitchell family was originally from Bellie, a small parish straddling western Banffshire and eastern Morayshire. It is interesting that the name Bellie is thought to be Gaelic in origin, being either a compound of the two Gaelic words Beul-aith, meaning 'the mouth of the ford', or less likely from Bellaidh, signifying 'broom.' The Mitchells moved to Uig, a district on the west side of Lewis, in 1827, where they farmed various areas of land. About 1860 the family moved to South Shawbost.

Opposite: John Mitchell stands proudly in the uniform of a First World War cavalry regiment.

John was one of a family of eight children, having five older brothers and two sisters who were younger. Not much is known about his childhood growing up on the croft, but no doubt he helped with the many tasks required on that small parcel of land. He also might have helped out with the fank, a big occasion in the village, going out to the moor in the early morning, and walking three or four miles, to gather the sheep and bring them in for shearing. He could also have taken part in the community effort of cutting peats and bringing them home as a supply of fuel.

As a typical child of a Hebridean village he spoke Gaelic. He probably never went hungry, but, as it has been described, life was almost on the edge – there was never any surplus. His diet would have been one of mainly fish – a big barrel of salt herring did all winter – and salted mutton. In addition there were hens, probably two cows, one for milking and one waiting to calf, providing the family with their own butter, cream and crowdie.

A move to London

At that time, many villages on the island had their own school, and John attended the local school in Shawbost. In the 1900s the minimum leaving age was only twelve, and while it is not recorded at what age John left school, he is thought to have been in his teens. He then tried to find work on the island, but was unsuccessful. Like many other islanders, he decided that he had to leave Lewis to find employment. While many Leòdhasaich (the Gaelic word for natives of Lewis), including some of his brothers and sisters, left the island for a new life in Canada or Australia, or sought work in Glasgow, John decided to head for London. Like many Lewismen, he left in the company of two others, one of whom went on to become head of the Glasgow Police Traffic Division.

Once in London he applied to join the Metropolitan Police and, being tall and well built, he was accepted as one of the 20,000 strong force. Not a great deal is known about his time in London, but it is thought he was posted to a station in the Golders Green area.

On the outbreak of the First World War John was called up and he was posted to a cavalry regiment, on account of his having had experience with horses. He was promoted initially to sergeant, finally becoming a commissioned Second Lieutenant. John was one of the fortunate ones to have survived the horrors of the War, suffering no more than a hand injury, losing three fingers.

John's second bus, an Overland built in 1922. The driver was Aonghas 'an Bhàn.

Return to Lewis

Although John must have been very aware that the employment situation on the island was no better than when he left, he returned to Lewis, perhaps with a longing for his native homeland. He must have considered the situation and decided that there was enough of a future in setting up a bus service on the island to justify the purchase of a vehicle in London. On being demobilised from the army in 1920 John bought his first bus, thought to be an American-built vehicle which had been converted from a wartime ambulance. It must have been quite an undertaking to drive the bus the 350 miles to Glasgow, where it would have been loaded on one of David MacBrayne's ships to convey it to Stornoway.

John Mitchell therefore became one of the first owners of a 'township bus' on the island. It was a very basic vehicle, fitted with wooden bench seats along each side. Gradually almost every village on the island acquired at least one of these, a small vehicle designed to carry both goods and between seven and fourteen passengers.

John returned to stay at the family home in Shawbost, and in January 1921 commenced running a daily (weekday) bus service from there to Stornoway, the main town on the island of Lewis. Rather than run to a fixed timetable the operator would run his bus as suited the people of the village, who might use the service to travel to work, for shopping in Stornoway or to connect with the steamer service to the mainland. The vehicle also acted as a delivery van, carrying all variety of goods, including tweeds, foodstuffs, materials for crofts, animals and mails. During the 1920s the number of these buses on the island increased considerably, although there was only one other service operating from Shawbost.

The introduction of John Mitchell's bus, and the few lorries operating in the area, led to the myth of the mysterious vehicle which was to be heard, but never seen, on the road between Shawbost and the neighbouring village of Dalmore. Eventually it was realised that the sound came from neither bus nor lorry, but was the sound of breakers crashing on the nearby beach. It was an example of superstition being created by the advance of technology – until John introduced his bus the sound of the sea could not be mistaken for anything else.

John Mitchell's uncle, Donald Maciver, known as 'Dondie', was the owner of the largest general merchants shop in Stornoway and also of Maciver's Garage at 15-17 Bayhead Street. In 1923 Donald asked his nephew to help run the garage business. John Mitchell had no hesitation in accepting the offer and was soon seen to be interested in developing the business. At that time there was no petrol depot on the island, and John took the opportunity to convert his original bus into a lorry to carry casks of petrol from the quay in Stornoway to the garage. He also saw that as more cars were appearing on the island a garage business would prosper, and he wanted to further develop the garage by knocking down the front office and opening up the garage entrance. Unfortunately, his uncle did not share his enthusiasm for the garage's potential, being solely interested in his merchant's shop, and he did not agree to this scheme. John, frustrated by this lack of progress, told his uncle that if he was unwilling to 'move with the times', then he would start up a garage business of his own. Donald Maciver's response was that he had no objections to that. However, only a few years later Donald died, and as his widow wished to maintain the garage business as it was, John Mitchell stayed on for another few years. During that time John took 'Jimsie' Afrin from school in 1927 to begin training as an apprentice mechanic; the two were to work together for many years.

Stornoway Gazette

IN SEARCH OF LEWIS

James Shaw Grant

Dannie Maciver's shop and garage [was where] I first met Johnny Mitchell. He had been in the Metropolitan Police I believe, for some years, before he returned to Shawbost and became one of the pioneers in the development of rural bus services. He then moved into town to take charge of the garage end of a cousin's business which was essentially a general merchants shop and Harris Tweed warehouse before branching into the new business of selling petrol and charging batteries for cars and for the new fangled wireless sets which were coming into vogue in the late Twenties.

There were no petrol pumps then. The precious fuel was tapped from a cask and poured from the gallon measure into the tank of the bus or car. Perhaps one should say 50 per cent went into the tank while the rest went into the gutter leaving Bayhead Street richly odoured with petrol fumes: the spirit of a new age. It was around this time Johnny Mitchell came back into the garage one day at lunchtime when his very able mechanic, Jimmy Munro, was at home for his meal. There was a raft of batteries being charged by a petrol engine and dynamo. Johnny saw that the acid was fizzing, indicating that the batteries were fully charged and would be damaged if the process went on too long. He switched the petrol engine off but it didn't stop. Puzzled he disconnected the pipe from the petrol tank but the engine still purred on. He was scratching his head in puzzlement, when Jimmy Munro returned, took in the situation at a glance, and slammed the switchboard with his fist. The engine stopped. Jimmy realised that the switch had jammed so that, when the engine was deprived of petrol, the whole apparatus began to run in reverse with the dynamo functioning as an electric motor powered by the well charged batteries. Johnny maintained his accustomed calm. "You know," he said, "For a moment I thought I had discovered perpetual motion." Even if he didn't discover perpetual motion, Johnny Mitchell was a shrewd businessman. He knew his cousin's shop was in decline, and the future lay with the motor car. Having failed to persuade his cousin to develop the growing end of the business, he "cut the painter" and set off on his own via the Golden Acre and the House of Lords to a prosperous business and an honourable mention in the Scottish law books.

At the same time, John's bus operations were proving successful, and two additional Overland buses were bought in 1922 and 1926. The second of these was purchased to replace the vehicle acquired in 1920, the last mentioned quite probably worn out by the daily travel over the unsurfaced Lewis roads. With two buses Mitchell would have been able to provide a daily service, even when one was off the road for repairs.

John Mitchell was tall, well built, and had a commanding presence. He was also known for being reserved, a quietly spoken man of few words, who listened closely to others, and acted astutely; behind it all there was a strong sense of character. His dry sense of humour was hidden from many, but was notable when it came out. In the years to come, his garage staff was very loyal to him, and he was known by many around the town and island.

In 1927, John Mitchell married Christina MacLean, or, as he described it in his own words, 'decided it was time to get married'. Like John, his wife was also from the West Side of Lewis: born in 1896, Christina was brought up in the village of North Bragar. After the wedding on 16 March 1927 at the Free Church of Scotland on Dee Street in Aberdeen, they set up their home in Stornoway.

Their first child, Christina (Chrissie) was born on 27 May 1928. She was followed by Neil Donald (Neil Dan), born on 15 March 1930. Sadly Neil Dan was only to live for five and a half months. That year was a tragic one for Christina; not only did she lose her infant son, but both her sister and her mother passed away. A second son, Ian Maclean, was born on 13 December 1933. It was he who would inherit the garage business from his father, and develop it until his retirement in 1995.

Top: An early photo of the Mitchell family. John's wife, Christina, is in the background, with Ian in front. Ian's sister, Chrissie, is held by Aggie Mackenzie, working as a nanny. She later became the first conductress.
Bottom: John Mitchell, his wife Christina and a young Ian pose on the running board of an early car.

2. MITCHELL'S TRANSPORT AND PARCELS SERVICE

By 1930 there were ten operators running buses from different villages to Stornoway. Two years later there were no fewer than 122; almost every village on the island now had a bus service. Operating a bus was a viable business, and provided an extremely useful service for the island's rural population. Before 1930 it was possible for anyone who wished to set up and run a bus service, which would explain this huge increase in numbers. During that year, however, the 1930 Road Traffic Act was passed and all bus operators on the island now had to be licensed. In the light of this, and his wish to set up in business on his own, in 1932 John Mitchell established 'Mitchell's Transport and Parcel Service.' The name of the company indicates the importance of the carriage of goods, supplying the inhabitants of the country districts with newspapers and parcels, with goods ordered from shops and businesses in Stornoway, as well as carrying passengers. John would also have provided a service to the growing number of weavers of Harris Tweed, delivering yarn and collecting woven tweeds as the industry began to expand. The first licence he obtained was for providing excursions and tours, but it must be assumed that this was for his Shawbost service as at this time he owned only two vehicles.

John Mitchell's original three buses had by now been disposed of and replaced by two new vehicles. The first of these, capable of carrying both passengers and freight, was a Bedford, and from this early association with that company, it did not take long for John to become the main dealer for Bedford for the whole island. Initially he rented a large shed on Esplanade Road, Stornoway, for use as a bus repair garage. The shed had been lying vacant, having previously been used as fish-curing premises. A second area of land with a small shed on Cromwell Street Quay was also being rented for a bus waiting room. John's business thrived. By 1934, his fleet comprised four 'coaches', two lorries and three private hire vehicles; two years later it had expanded to six 'coaches', four lorries and four private hire vehicles.

As part of his garage business, John Mitchell was involved in both supplying buses and in building bodies for vehicles for various operators on the island. These included an early Overland bus,

THE ROAD TRAFFIC ACT 1930

The 1930 Act was the result of concern in the early 1920s for public safety, the government hoping to reduce accident levels. Intervention on these grounds led on to further examination and eventual control of other aspects of the industry. Hence, the early 1920s discussions on the safety aspects of road passenger industry were crucial to the development of the regulation incorporated in the 1930 Road Traffic Act. One of the most remarkable aspects of the 1930 quantity licensing legislation is the way in which it lasted, despite the faulty premises underpinning it, almost without change for fifty years.

With regard to public service vehicles the legislation introduced the following:

- Central regulation of bus and coach services throughout the United Kingdom – this included the classification of different types of public service vehicles.

- Introduction of a 30-mile-an-hour speed limit for buses and coaches.

- The requirement of licences for public service vehicles, drivers and conductors.

- Rules regarding the conduct of drivers, conductors and passengers on public service vehicles.

- Limitation of hours of continuous driving.

- The setting up of Traffic Areas and Traffic Commissioners; the duties of the Traffic Commissioners included the granting of licences for any particular route applied for, and the setting of timetables and fares.

supplied new in 1927 to Peter Macaulay of Carloway, who also purchased a new Bedford in 1935. In 1933, new Bedford buses were supplied to Donald Mackenzie of Portnaguran and John Macleod of Portvoller. Two bodies, a twelve-seat and a fourteen seat, on a Bedford and Dodge chassis respectively, were purchased in 1934 and 1938 by Peter Macritchie of Ardroil, while John Murdo Morrison, based in Gravir, ordered two bodies from John, both to be fitted on Bedford chassis, in 1933 and 1939.

John Mitchell also built bodies for his own fleet. Two were built on Albion chassis in 1936, while five were made for Bedfords between 1938 and 1947.

John Mitchell realised that the future lay in providing services for the growing number of motorists on the island, and in 1932 he was actively looking for a more suitable site to develop a garage business. His eye was drawn to the area of land between Matheson Road and Bayhead Street, Stornoway. It was an ideal site for his requirements: space for a large garage and showroom, with room for petrol pumps and storage space for buses. He sent a letter to Mr Edwin Aldred, the Factor of the Stornoway Trust, expressing his interest in the land. The story of what followed is described in the next chapter.

In June 1935, he applied to the Harbour Commission for permission to erect a petrol pump in close proximity to his office on Cromwell Street Quay. The application was refused, after discovering that there was a water main and a sewer in the vicinity. A suggestion was made to accommodate John Mitchell by offering him an alternative piece of land, a triangular area of ground at the Bayhead entrance to Cromwell Street Quay, which was used for no purpose at all except 'dressing an odd spar,' and which was bringing in no revenue.

John Mitchell consequently applied to the Harbour Commission at their next meeting for permission to erect a petrol pump on that piece of land. Once again permission was not granted. While one Commissioner argued for the pump, as increased petrol sales would also mean more income for the Commission as all petrol entered the island though the port, it was pointed out that the Town Council would not allow a petrol pump being erected which had a swinging arm which would cross the pavement, and it was the Town Council which would have the final say.

'A suburban service of buses'

John Mitchell started to operate his first regular local service (known officially as a stage carriage service) in May 1933. The licence was for a circular service in Stornoway; this would have been a short route, as the town at that time did not extend beyond Matheson Road. This was a new development in Stornoway's transport facilities, described in the Stornoway Gazette as 'the institution of a suburban service of buses.' The half-hourly service between Stornoway and its suburbs was said to 'ensure that the town will have more modern transport facilities than many places of a similar size on the mainland.'

John Mitchell stated that his desire was to educate the people of Stornoway to do their shopping and pleasure excursions by bus instead of by post as had been the custom. To publicise his new service he placed a notice in the Stornoway Gazette on 26 May, which stated,

> 'Mr John Mitchell begs to intimate that his suburban bus service will commence next month. The bus will run at regular intervals from Sandwick Cross to Laxdale Bridge via Newton Street and Cromwell Street.
>
> 'As Mr Mitchell is anxious to meet the convenience of the public as far as possible he would be pleased to learn by letter or otherwise from workmen, schoolchildren, etc., who intend to take advantage of the service, what hours would be most convenient for them.'

The licence for this service had been granted by the Traffic Commissioners for only a month, and shortly after John Mitchell applied successfully to continue the run. He also introduced a new service to Sandwick, Melbost, Steinish, Goathill and the Golf Course, which at this time was located immediately beyond Melbost.

At the same time, in a further example of how the bus services were for the benefit of the people, John Mitchell was granted, along with other operators, permission to temporarily apply variations in his services to meet the needs of fishermen. This was because it was the start of the fishing season and the fishermen and their assistants had to travel between their homes and Stornoway to prepare their boats and gear.

Excursions and further afield

Although still only owning three buses, Mr Mitchell put his excursion licence to good use during the summer of 1933. During July he offered a number of tours, advertised in the Stornoway Gazette using the slogan 'See Lewis First by Mitchell's Charabanc.' A different destination was offered each day: Lemreway on Mondays, Butt of Lewis on Tuesdays, Uig on Wednesdays, Tarbert on Thursdays and to Callanish on Fridays. The cost of each tour varied between 7/6d and 9/6d. The Golf Course was served on Wednesdays and Saturdays;

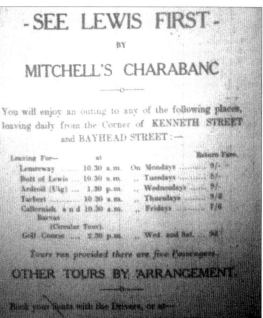

Top: A bank holiday outing.
Bottom left: John offered tours to various parts of the island on the Autumn Holiday in 1933.
Bottom right: Tours to a variety of destinations were advertised to run in the summer of 1933.

the fare for this service was 9d. The tours would operate if there were a minimum of five passengers. 'Mitchell's Charabanc Tours' also advertised special 'All-day Tours,' from 10am to 10pm, to Tarbert, Uig and Ness, to run on 7 August, the Autumn Holiday Monday. With two meals provided, the cost for one of these excursions was 14/6d.

It would appear that buses would also be run to a variety of local beaches on good summer days. One Stornoway resident described how 'The enterprising Mr John Mitchell ran buses on very good days to nearby beaches. This was a great boon as there were few cars in Stornoway. Our favourite outing was to the lovely Melbost beach by the old golf course. Of course the sky and the sea were always blue.'

In 1934 John Mitchell introduced a twice weekly service to the south of Harris, commencing on 2 July. Advertised as being operated by 'Mitchell's Transport Services' the service was scheduled to run from 'Mitchell's Transport Office,' in Stornoway to Rodel every Monday and Thursday, leaving Stornoway at 9.30am and returning from Rodel at 3pm. The fare structure was interesting: a single fare outward was 11/-, while an inward journey cost only 10/-; a return ticket provided a big saving as it only cost 15/-. This service must have proved a success as the following year it was increased to operate on a daily basis.

The success of his services prompted John Mitchell to apply to the Town Council in 1934 to change the temporary building on Cromwell Street Quay he used as a transport and parcels office to a permanent structure. It was understood that this was where his excursions and other trips would leave from. While it was agreed that there was no doubt that a parcels office was a public necessity, it was thought by some that a better site could be found, one which had a better location with less danger arising from congestion. The request, however, was duly granted.

The town council also gave permission for John to convert the yard he occupied on the Esplanade for use as a garage. Later that year, John received a request to refrain from parking his buses on Cromwell Street Quay, beyond the limits of his bus station. This seemed to be slightly unfair as it was pointed out by John that 'every day of the week twenty or thirty buses' belonging to other operators were parked on South Beach Street.

Further expansion of John's bus operations continued to take place. A service to Ness was introduced, although the exact date when this started is not clear. In 1936 a service from Stornoway to Back was operated, but less than a year later this was substituted by a service to Tong. This was the result of John Mitchell taking over the licence and service from Norman Macdonald of Tong, who had operated the service from 1931 with two small buses. This was the first of a number of small operators who were taken over by Mitchell, allowing him to increase both the range of services and the size of his bus fleet. This numbered six by 1938, and continued to grow over the following years.

In 1938 Mitchell branched out into the Point area, to the east of Stornoway, by acquiring the licence and service from Stornoway to Portnaguran, provided by Donald Mackenzie of Portnaguran. This service did not survive beyond August 1939. Four other routes were introduced that year. An extension to North Tolsta was made of the Tong service, and the service to Harris was split into two, one to Leverburgh and the other to Rodel. The fourth new route was a service from Stornoway to Melbost.

Dealings with the Traffic Commissioners

All the new services introduced by John Mitchell had to be approved and licensed by the Traffic Commissioners. This was carried out by the Traffic Commissioners for Scotland, who once or twice every year would visit the island and hold meetings to hear applications to operate bus services. John Mitchell was a regular attender on these occasions, both to put the case for his own new services and to object to others. On most occasions matters were straightforward: objections were raised when a new service was thought to be in direct competition with an existing route, but as will be seen John Mitchell sometimes had other ideas and he could introduce some unusual arguments. So well-known was his attendance at these meetings that at the 1953 meeting the Chairman, Mr Robertson, remarked jocularly to John when he arrived a few minutes late, 'We thought you weren't coming, Mr Mitchell, and we were on the point of refusing your applications.'

At the 1933 meeting things went well for John Mitchell. Objections were raised regarding the fares he charged on his service to Sandwick and Laxdale. It was claimed that they were only half that of other operators who were in direct competition. John responded, saying that his service was very much appreciated by the public, especially workmen and schoolchildren, for whom he was hoping to arrange special concessions as done on the mainland. The secretary of the Golf Club supported John's new service to the Golf Course, stating that at present there was no service to the course, and that it would add to their membership, while assisting the people of Stornoway and visitors to the island, who had complained of the difficulty of getting to the Golf Course.

Top left: In July 1933 a twice weekly service was introduced from Stornoway to Tarbert. Top right: John Mitchell carries out roadside repairs for a lady driver. Middle left: John at the wheel of an early car. One of the passengers is Andrew Henderson, whose father was also one of the pioneers of the motor trade on the island. Middle right: In September 1933 this advertisement appeared in the Stornoway Gazette. Bottom left: John was selling new cars in 1933. Bottom right: A fine example of the type of bodies built by John in the 1930s. This Bedford bus was owned by Peter Macritchie of Ardroil who operated a service from Uig to Stornoway.

In 1934 there were applications for over one hundred bus services in the Outer Hebrides from a similar number of operators. Most of these were granted without question, but one in particular, involving John Mitchell, led to some discussion. It concerned the service to Back. The Traffic Commissioner pointed out that there had been a complaint about the 'gangway of the car being obstructed by haddock, over which anyone entering or leaving had to step.' He added, 'If haddock were to be carried they must be in a sack.' John Mitchell replied that passengers were never carried when there was haddock, except the fishwives to whom the haddock belonged. There was no mention of the outcome of this complaint, but it is clear that discussions at the Commissioners' meetings ranged from the serious to the trivial.

The service to Harris attracted some attention at the meetings held in 1936. On Mondays and Thursdays John Mitchell ran a bus from Stornoway to Rodel and return. The success of this service prompted him to apply to the Traffic Commissioners the following year for a daily service. The application was opposed by seven operators in Harris. John claimed that the service was in the public interest and should be granted. In fact only two of the objectors would be materially affected by the proposed service, and it was suggested their timetables could be altered 'to allow them to run a little in front of Mr Mitchell's service'. The application was granted.

At the next meeting the situation was reversed. A rival application to run a similar service was made to which John Mitchell objected. The proposed service aimed to allow a return trip from the south of Harris to Stornoway in one day, and would also be of convenience in meeting the mail steamer in Tarbert. Mr Mitchell said that the new service would make his uneconomic. The Chairman of the Commissioners pointed out that John was the 'pioneer of the service' and had 'rendered a great public service to the community.' It ran all year, 'in fair weather and in foul.' He considered it unfair that the new service should cut in front of Mr Mitchell's and 'try to take the cream of the traffic.' This traffic was certainly not great, as John showed in his defence. During the winter he picked up about two passengers per day and during the short summer season his average was about eight. He claimed the service could not be maintained without the mail and parcels contracts. Finally he added that he had received nothing but praise for his service. His words must have carried the day for the application was refused.

3. MITCHELL v THE STORNOWAY TRUSTEES

As mentioned in Chapter 2, John Mitchell's business had prospered and grown to the extent that it became evident that his existing premises on Esplanade Road would quickly become too small and restrictive, and that he would need to find larger premises. Accordingly, on 23 December 1932, he submitted an application to feu [rent] an area of vacant ground at the corner of Matheson Road and Bayhead Street in Stornoway. The application was to lead to a major court case which was not resolved until July 1936.

The land was the property of the Stornoway Trust, a publicly owned Estate, created in 1923 when the estate formerly owned by Lord Leverhulme was gifted by him to the community when he left the island. John Mitchell initially sent a letter to the Factor of the Trustees, Mr Aldred, stating his interest in the plot of land for the purpose of building a public garage on it. John's letter enquired whether the Trustee Committee would be willing to feu him the site. The application was discussed at the next meeting of the Trustees in January 1933. Considerable time was spent discussing the application, mainly on the desirability or otherwise of maintaining an open space at the entrance to the Lews Castle Policies, as the Castle Grounds were then described. A Trustee enquired as to whether any building plans had been submitted, to which the reply was, 'At this stage plans would not be necessary.' This was countered by the comment, 'While not wishing to obstruct the business, I must say I am surprised at that ruling. Before our application [for a different building] was considered we had to produce plans.' It was then stated, 'If the site is granted we will require to see plans before the building is erected.' It will be seen that the submission of plans was to play a significant part in the ensuing court case.

During the discussion it was also noted that a previous, similar application for the site had been turned down because of its location. It was also pointed out by a Trustee who had visited the site, that Mr Mitchell intended to build his property near the back of the area, so that there would be no blind corner created. It was a triangular piece of land, and he was going to build at the base so there would be nothing near the point of the area, except the petrol pump. Another Trustee said that the piece of ground was lying waste and it would be beneficial if a garage was built there.

In the House of Lords.

ON APPEAL

(FROM THE SECOND DIVISION OF THE COURT OF SESSION
IN SCOTLAND.)

ALEXANDER MACLENNAN and OTHERS (The Trustees acting
under Deed of Trust by the Right Honourable William
Hesketh, Viscount Leverhulme of the Western Isles) . . *Appellants.*

JOHN MITCHELL . . . . *Respondent.*

PETITION OF APPEAL.
APPELLANTS' CASE.
RESPONDENT'S CASE.

ANDERSON MacARTHUR & CO.,
Solicitors,
30 Francis Street, Stornoway.

ALEX. MORISON & CO., W.S.,
33 Queen Street, Edinburgh.

BEVERIDGE & CO.,
23 Abingdon Street,
Westminster, London, S.W.1,
Appellants' Agents.

BORLAND KING & SHAW,
Writers,
95 West George Street, Glasgow, C.2.

DOVE LOCKHART & SMART, S.S.C.
29 York Place, Edinburgh.

INCE, ROSCOE, WILSON & GLOVER,
Solicitors,
10–11 Lime Street, London, E.C.3.
Respondent's Agents.

The title page and the first page of the transcript of the appeal in the House of Lords in 1936.

In the House of Lords.

(From the Second Division of the Court of Session in Scotland.)

ALEXANDER MACLENNAN, Retired Merchant, Bellevue, Goathill Road, Stornoway . . . . . .

WILLIAM JOHN TOLMIE, Chemist, 49 Matheson Road, Stornoway

RODERICK SMITH, Chemist, 9 James Street, Stornoway . .

ALEXANDER JOHN MACKENZIE, Tweed Manufacturer, Springfield, Matheson Road, Stornoway . . . .

MRS. JULIA MARTIN FRASER, The Old House, Frances Street, Stornoway, being respectively the Provost, Magistrates and two Councillors of the Burgh of Stornoway, the *ex officio* Trustees, and

KENNETH MACDONALD, School Teacher, Thistlecroft, Sandwick, by Stornoway . . . . . .

COLIN SCOTT MACKENZIE, Solicitor, 8 Matheson Road, Stornoway

MURDO MACLEOD, Merchant, 71 Kenneth Street, Stornoway .

OSSIAN MACASKILL, Blacksmith, 53 Seaforth Road, Stornoway, and

DONALD JOHN MACKENZIE, Painter, 27 Kenneth Street, Stornoway, the elected Trustees acting under Deed of Trust granted by the Right Honourable William Hesketh, Viscount Leverhulme of the Western Isles, dated 12th November 1923, and registered in the Books of Council and Session 21st January 1924 . . .

Appellants (Defenders).

JOHN MITCHELL, 70 Kenneth Street, Stornoway . . .

Respondent (Pursuer).

PETITION AND APPEAL

MORRISON & GIBB LIMITED, Printers, Edinburgh.

Various arguments for and against the application were then aired. One Trustee considered that it was the best corner in the town, the ground having been laid out 'by a lady [Lady Matheson] whose taste had never been approached by her successors,' and it should therefore be preserved as open space. Another Trustee said that the site was not a beauty spot at present but it might be made one. It was further proposed that rather than grant the present application, that John Mitchell could be offered a different site on the Bayhead embankment, which he had previously applied for, or that an alternative site might be found between Matheson Road and Plantation Road. A more neutral view was offered that 'so far as open spaces were concerned it was not going to make much difference whether they had a garage or the present state of affairs at that corner.' It was thought that this would be an opportunity of 'decentralising the motor traffic' and from that point of view the application was worth considering.

Further discussion considered the type of building to be erected. It was thought that it was as easy to build a beautiful garage as a beautiful grocer's shop or a beautiful dwelling house, and they could insist that the garage was in keeping with the immediate surroundings. Macrae and Dick's garage in Dingwall was mentioned as an example of a garage which did not spoil the appearance of the surroundings, being described as one of the finest buildings in that town. Further discussion included the suggestion that if the people of Stornoway were asked to vote on the matter there would be an 'overwhelming majority against it.' The capability of the Bayhead sewer to cope with extra capacity was also used to put the case against the application.

After this division of opinion, the matter of the application was put to a vote. The result was five votes cast in favour and four against – John Mitchell had his application for the garage approved. Mr Aldred then informed John by letter on 16 January 1933 of the discussions which had taken place and that the Trustees were offering to feu him the ground at an annual cost of £12 per acre. Mr Mitchell was also requested to supply the Trust with a site plan. On 20 January, John replied, describing the grounds as requested and asking for the feu charter [a document outlining the terms of the feu agreement] for his own records; a site plan was not included with John's letter.

As soon as the matter became public knowledge, those against the proposal were not slow in voicing their disapproval. Two letters printed in the Stornoway Gazette on the two following weeks expressed their disfavour in no uncertain terms. Emotive phrases such as, '[it] should be maintained for all time as an open space', 'it is the duty of our citizens to see that our town is beautified' and 'neither

Lady Matheson nor the late Lord Leverhulme would ever have dreamt of handing over the space to be used in the manner proposed' were backed up by more factual arguments. These mentioned congestion of traffic, and the unsuitability of the existing water supply and sewage provision.

A further letter opined that before the Trustees granted the feu they should have let other traders in the town know of the availability of the site, and by advertising this, the true value of the land would have been realised.

The Trustees met again on 27 January, when the topic of the Bayhead site was again discussed. This centred on how much of the site was required, and whether a road was to be put through the site for accommodating cars waiting for petrol, which was thought welcome to prevent congestion. The question of the provision of a pavement was also discussed, and the Trustees took account of the letters in the Gazette. Finally, having been reminded that a majority of the Trustees voted for granting the feu the last time, the meeting finally voted unanimously that feu be granted, except for two amendments to allow for a six-foot pavement and rounding off the corner in a satisfactory way. John Mitchell, as a member of the public, attended the meeting, and he would therefore have been aware of these amendments, although they were not explained in a letter from Mr Aldred to John Mitchell sent on 1 February.

On 3 February, John Mitchell and Mr Aldred met to set the boundaries for the production of the site plan, and one week later the Trustees were presented with the plans, which they approved. The following day Mr Aldred met with John and his surveyor on site to take measurements, in accordance with the amendments regarding the pavement and corner. On 13 February, John Mitchell's completed plans were received by Mr Aldred. The same day John made an appearance before the Stornoway Dean of Guild Court to petition for the building of a public garage. [At that time the Dean of Guild Court served the function which is today carried out by a planning department of a local council, viz. the approving of planning permission]. John duly confirmed he was the proprietor of the land, as he truthfully believed he was, and submitted two copies of the approved plans. The court accepted the petition and permission was granted, with the usual time for objections to be lodged, that being before 27 February.

On 15 February the Guild Court asked the Trustees to confirm that the land would be rented by John Mitchell, as per their feu agreement, which they duly did. It would seem that the way was clear for John to go ahead with the garage.

John Mitchell then travelled to Glasgow on 19 February to meet with the Glasgow Steel Roofing Company, with whom he finalised a contract for the erection of his garage. He did this on the understanding that the garage had been approved.

The proposed building did not appear on the agenda for the Trustees' meeting on 24 February. However, at that meeting the Trustees departed from the agenda to address complaints regarding the garage site from other rate payers. As a result of this, the Trust Committee voted to withdraw the feu contract from John Mitchell. The Guild Court was also informed of the decision and accordingly dismissed his petition. When John returned from Glasgow he received a letter from Mr Aldred stating that the feu agreement had been revoked and John's petition had been refused.

In the light of all this, it is not surprising that John Mitchell's next action was to write to the Trust on 4 March, requesting that the granting of the feu be reinstated. The Trustees next met on 17 March to discuss the legal advice they had been given regarding John's claim; the legal advice suggested that the feu should be reinstated, which was not the opinion they were seeking. The Trustees voted against the advice.

Legal Proceedings are begun

The next stage in the proceedings took place on 4 September 1933, when John Mitchell began legal proceedings against the Stornoway Trust, seeking to uphold the feu agreement the two parties had originally reached. This was heard in Edinburgh at the Court of Session in the Outer House the following year. [The Outer House is one of two parts of the Scottish Court of Session, the supreme civil court in Scotland.] Not surprisingly, the matter was on the agenda of the next meeting of the Trust, when a considerable portion of the meeting was occupied with a discussion 'in camera' (in private) of Counsel's opinion of the action raised by John Mitchell.

The action was heard in the Court of Session on 26 and 27 June 1934 and on 12 and 13 July 1934. The case centred round the confusion caused by the letter of 1 February 1933 in which the Trustees stated they were prepared to feu the site, but with certain reservations. John Mitchell argued that this letter constituted a contract, serving as acceptance by the Trustees, and that the reservations contained in it did not constitute a counter offer to which he had to respond. He therefore went ahead with his trip to Glasgow where he incurred considerable expense in the belief that the contract had been agreed upon. The Trustees, however, considered the contract to be still under consideration.

John further argued that the Trustees had entered into a valid contract and the contract had been homologated [approved by a body of officials such as the Dean of Guild Court], and that he had incurred considerable financial outlay in the belief of the contract's validity. The Trustees responded that there was no written contract and they were therefore entitled to withdraw, that John Mitchell's expenses had been incurred before the agreement of the contract and therefore could not influence the outcome, and that John Mitchell had not approved the contract, as he had not signed either the site plan or the building plan.

The judgement made by Lord Wark was delivered on 13 July 1934. He considered that John Mitchell's expenditure did not imply that a contract had been made and that in fact no contract existed. The decision went in favour of the Stornoway Trust Committee, freeing them from any contract.

The decision is appealed

John Mitchell then appealed to the Inner House of the Court of Session. This court hears appeals from the Outer House; the cases are heard by three judges, with their decisions based on a majority verdict. The appeal was heard on 30 and 31 January, 1 and 5 February 1935. Two of the three judges found in favour of John Mitchell. They considered that the contract had been homologated and therefore the Trustees should have been barred from leaving their obligations as they had in fact broken the contract. The third judge believed that there was no written contract and that neither party were bound to the agreement. Thus on 15 March 1935, on a judgement of two against one, the court decided to recall Lord Wark's decision and found in favour of John Mitchell. It was also concluded that there should be a payment to John Mitchell of '£3,000 in respect of loss and damage in consequence of the defenders' (the Trustees) delay in implementing the agreement.'

To the House of Lords

This was not the end of the matter. At the April 1935 meeting of the Stornoway Trust Committee the members met 'in camera' [in private] to discuss the Court's decision. It was agreed to instruct their Edinburgh agents to take the necessary steps to lodge an appeal with the House of Lords in London. The House of Lords, in addition to its legislative responsibility, also functioned at that time as a court of last resort. Cases are heard by five judges, with decisions based on a majority verdict.

On 7 May 1936, the Trustees formally appealed to the House of Lords against the Inner House of the Court of Session's decision. The case was heard over six days in May 1936. After the first morning's hearing one of the judges, Lord Macmillan, became indisposed. The parties agreed to continue the hearing before the other four judges, but after the arguments had continued for almost another day and a half, it was intimated that the judges regarded the issue raised to be of such importance that they wished all five judges to be present. After an adjournment, the case was continued, and it was mentioned that the length of the case was due to two factors: the importance of the legal issues raised and the indisposition of Lord Macmillan.

The Verdict

The five judges gave their verdict on 22 July 1936. Unanimously, they considered that the letters seemed to indicate that both parties had reached agreement, concluding that the case should be dismissed with costs being awarded to John Mitchell. After just over three and a half years, John had won his battle for the Bayhead site – and the court's decision also defined important legal precedents in Contract Law.

The Stornoway Gazette reported: 'Unanimous verdict for Mitchell, with full expenses— a few minutes after the arrival of the telegram, on Wednesday last, with the decision of the House of Lords in the now notorious "Mitchell Case," the news went round the town like wildfire. The majority of the general public seemed pleased that Mr Mitchell had succeeded, and he received many congratulatory handshakes. Bailie Tolmie and Councillor Macaskill, having supported his application from the first, and opposed the legal proceedings, naturally felt that the result vindicated their views, but other prominent citizens, in close touch with Local Government affairs in town, viewed the decision with consternation. Apart from the rights and wrongs of the case, they saw the people of Stornoway faced with the problem of raising a prince's ransom to meet the costs.'

£3,000 damages were due to John Mitchell from the Stornoway Trust, as well as the Trust's legal expenses, thought to be a considerable sum; in addition, in the event of the Trustees refusing to hand over the feu, there would be additional damages of £5,000. At the next meeting of the Trustees, in August 1936, the Factor, Mr Aldred, intimated that copies of the Draft judgement and Final judgement had been received, and that John Mitchell's Edinburgh Agents had written to enquire whether the Trustees intended to give John his Feu Charter, and asking for a copy of the Charter. It was agreed that the matter should be discussed at a later date, and at their next meeting

Top: One of the floats in the 1937 Stornoway Carnival, which was raising funds for building an extension to the island's hospital, was clearly inspired by the expense of the Court case. Bottom: Lord Leverhulme's fish processing plant at Leverburgh, Harris. It was from here that John obtained his first garage building.

the Trustees unanimously agreed to grant the Charter for the feu. Provost Smith opined, 'We must be prepared to shift our ground in new circumstances, and do the legal thing, quite apart from our own opinions and feelings.'

Looking for the legal costs

The November 1936 meeting of the Stornoway Trustees was described in the Stornoway Gazette as being 'short and sweet.' It was even noted that, 'the Trustees had found time to have some entertaining Gaelic stories from George Macleod during a pause in the proceedings'. In one way, however, the meeting was not sweet. The Trustees were confronted with a bill for £500/1/9d [£500.8p] for their own legal expenses in the House of Lords appeal. The Trust had already paid, as decreed in the case, John Mitchell's expenses in the appeal, this amounting to £657/18/8d [£657.93p]. They had also spent about £1,100 in connection with earlier stages in the litigation. The total expenses that the Trustees would incur amounted to about £3,200. The question was raised, 'Can we pay it?' The Factor replied that it was a case of having to pay it. It was then suggested that the matter be postponed until the December meeting, which was the end of their financial year. Another Trustee thought, 'there was no good in delaying the evil day,' but it was decided to leave the matter until the following meeting.

In December, payment was sanctioned to cover the Trust's own legal expenses. They still had to deal with John Mitchell's expenses. 'This is like throwing salt in the sea,' commented one Trustee. As it was the second meeting at which the matter had arisen, it was decided that all payments be made. Fortunately, as the Factor reported, the Trust was able to meet the account.

At the same meeting, a draft Feu charter was approved for submission to John Mitchell's Law Agents. Even this was not passed without comment, a Trustee stating, 'I am not going to sit here and be a party to accepting any draft without knowing the details. I am not going to sign away any of the electors' inheritance without knowing what it is about.' The draft was then read and approved with minor alterations. The draft stated that the site was to be used solely for the erection of a motor garage, that the buildings were to be subject to approval, and that Mr Mitchell was duty bound to make a six foot path all round and to erect a dwarf wall and railing.

Finally, at the meeting of the Trustees held in April 1937 the terms of the charter were approved and the Bayhead Garage Feu Charter was signed. At last after three and a half years, John Mitchell could proceed with the construction of his garage.

Letter to Stornoway Gazette, 3 February 1933. This letter was written just before the initial appeal was heard by the Court of Session. It must be assumed that "The Feuar" is John Mitchell.

BAYHEAD GARAGE SITE

Sir, - The haggling of the Stornoway Trustees over the Bayhead Garage site during the past few weeks must have provided a source of considerable amusement to readers of the 'Stornoway Gazette.'

As we all know, this site was granted in the usual way, and went through all the stages, including the submitting, approving, granting and signing of the feuar's proposed building plans. To all intents and purposes the Trustees had now finally disposed of this business.

But not realising their responsibilities to the public and their office they decided at a later date to violate their Standing Orders by going back on their decision. The Trustees appear to be very anxious that the feuar should concentrate on an alternative garage site without considering the congestion, annoyance and the danger in the number of increased accidents which would inevitably result if any of the alternative sites proposed were approved of.

Regarding the so-called influential petition, I maintain that no matter where a man decides to build a garage within the burgh boundaries, it is an easy matter to obtain seventy odd signatures of people anxious to oppose him.

The most amazing thing, however, concerning the Trustees withdrawing their grant of this site is the fact that in my opinion it is an ideal spot for a garage both from the point of view of the moving public and the motorists in our Island. In this respect its equal cannot be found in the town of Stornoway.

I feel, therefore, that the Trustees have laid themselves open to severe censure in obstructing a measure which would provide a useful and needed service.

 A small minority means to lay stress on the beauty of this small and trifling plot of ground; it is also evident that any beauty it can lay claim to was blankly ignored until the feuar was seen to be making faces at it.

Without stressing the arguments for and against the beauty of the plot in question, surely any alteration made in the landscape would be more than compensated for by the much-needed improvement of the amenities the creation of a modern garage would provide.

THE FEUAR

The Stornoway Gazette's view

In addition to reporting the court's verdict, the Stornoway Gazette's editorial of 31 July 1936 noted: 'A dispute which could have been settled amicably, out of court, if an accommodating spirit had prevailed, has been fought out in the highest Court in the land, after a process of litigation costing thousands of pounds – and the decision now given is based not on the moral rights and wrongs of the case, not on the requirements of public policy in Stornoway, but on a technicality which few people profess to understand.'

The editorial went on to state, 'The only actors in the drama who have done well are the lawyers,' adding that, 'There is not much consolation to be drawn from the knowledge that "Mitchell v. the Stornoway Trustees" may achieve a legal immortality, as an illustration of the opinion of the House of Lords on "rei interventu" [sic] and "homologation" [legal principles of breach of contract].'

The editorial also considered that the practice of canvassing individuals rather than publicly advertising rent opportunities, was not one which should be continued for public business, commenting, 'the evils which proceed from canvassing (of which this is but a single example) are the fault not of those who practice it, for they are merely looking after their proper interests, but of the public bodies which permit it.' Another lesson which should have been learned from the case was 'the danger of deciding matters which involve general principles without relation to the principles themselves. It was on the general principle of maintaining the amenities of the town that the Trustees decided to withdraw Mr Mitchell's feu, after granting it, and yet the Trustees at no time had before them any document, or previous funding of their own, on the question of town planning.' Indeed, it was not all that long after the case that the Town Council initiated town planning schemes.

Another consideration arising from the case was the cost to the Stornoway Trust, and how they were going to meet this. 'A cynic may derive some satisfaction from the thought that since the Trust has never fulfilled the philanthropic objects for which it was founded, the community will lose nothing tangible. But the time was within sight this year when the Trust could show a clear balance sheet, and begin to disburse funds for social purposes. That day has now been postponed indefinitely; the "Mitchell Case" will not bankrupt the Trust, but it will leave it saddled with debt probably for a decade.'

In conclusion, the editor wrote, 'one can only add that Mr Mitchell, in his various undertakings, has shown initiative and enterprise, from which the community has sometimes benefited as well as he. Now that his right has been so signally vindicated, it is to be hoped that he will lay out his valuable piece of ground in a manner to confound his critics.'

4. THE GARAGE IS BUILT

Having finally obtained the land at the corner of Bayhead and Matheson Road, the way was now clear for John Mitchell to construct his garage. As it would have involved considerable expense to import all the materials for the garage from the mainland, John looked around to see what was available on the island, and identified a large metal-framed building lying empty and unused at Leverburgh, at the south end of Harris. This building had been constructed in 1920 as part of Lord Leverhulme's plan to turn the village of Obbe, which he renamed Leverburgh, into a major fishing centre. Over 300 men had been involved in preparing the site and constructing an accommodation block, curing sheds, smoke houses and a refrigeration building. Work huts, store sheds and a twenty car garage were added to this development, and houses were built for a team of managers. After the death of Lord Leverhulme in 1925, the executors and the Board of Lever Brothers had no interest in the Leverburgh project and they ordered the work to cease and the work force to be laid off. They put the South Harris Estate up for sale and in October 1925 the pier site at Leverburgh was sold for £5,000. Since that time the buildings had lain empty.

The structure of the curing shed looked ideal to John Mitchell for his requirements, and he was able to purchase the building. There was, however, one major problem: the building was located some sixty miles to the south of Stornoway, separated not just by the steep Harris hills but by a narrow, poorly surfaced winding road. Nor was the building of a lightweight construction; if anything, it had been over-engineered, perhaps to withstand the rigours of Hebridean winter gales. The weight of one pillar was measured in tons, and there was no possibility of transporting either them or the solid beams overland. Added to these difficulties was the fact that there was no crane on the island which was strong enough to deal with the dismantling.

John was not to be deterred by these difficulties. His answer to the problem was to build rafts, both strong enough and large enough to carry the heavy weight of the beams. Over the following weeks the rafts made many trips up the Minch from Leverburgh to Stornoway, towed very slowly by a local fishing boat. Not one piece of the building was lost at sea and eventually, using a huge sheerlegs [a floating vessel fitted with a crane] to unload the rafts at Stornoway, the structure was successfully assembled on Bayhead Street.

By 1938, the construction of his garage and vehicle showroom was complete, and from this site John Mitchell proceeded both to develop his garage business and run his bus operations. The site first appeared in the valuation role in 1938, described as 'garage and petrol tanks' and with a rateable value of £40. John continued to maintain the connection he had made previously with Bedford Vehicles and he was soon able to obtain a Vauxhall Bedford franchise.

In the same year, an area of land adjoining the new garage site became available, and John Mitchell submitted a petition for its feu, which was duly obtained, although it did not appear in the valuation roll until 1945.

A second piece of land on Esplanade Road, adjacent to Quay Street, was also rented by John Mitchell from 1940. Described as a 'yard and stores,' it had previously been used as a coal yard by James M Mackenzie. The valuation roll shows that John Mitchell gave up the tenancy of the two sites on Esplanade Road in 1948.

5. EXCURSION BY BOAT

John's entrepreneurial talents extended beyond the garage, cars and buses. As well as organising coach tours and excursions during the summer he also had a small boat which was available for trips or excursions to places such as Arnish, near the lighthouse at the entrance to Stornoway Harbour. These boat trips were offered between 1935 and 1937. In the latter year they probably ceased to operate as a result of John Mitchell appearing in a court case in August 1937. The charge was that 'he was the *owner* [italics added] of a motor boat which carried more than twelve passengers [and] did proceed on an excursion without having a certificate from the Board of Trade in respect of the boat.'

The excursion in question took place on Coronation Day, 12 May 1937. In court, the Deputy Superintendent of Marine at Leith stated that while he was stationed in Stornoway during May he noticed a crowd around a boat tied up at Esplanade Quay. He saw that the boat was about to set off on an excursion. He counted the number of people on the vessel and discovered there were thirty-four, one of whom seemed to be in charge. Knowing that there were no passenger boats registered in Stornoway he was immediately suspicious.

John Mitchell explained that in 1935 he did not apply for a certificate to carry more than twelve passengers because the expense was too great. He would have had to pay the cost of bringing a surveyor from Glasgow and the cost of the certificate as well. In addition, John's solicitor stated that on no occasion between June 1935 and May 1936 did he know of John Mitchell's boat carrying more than the permitted twelve.

John at the tiller of his boat. Middle: John takes a group for a picnic on his boat, but with no overloading this time. Right: John is pictured here with Captain John Smith on the mail boat *Loch Seaforth*.

On this occasion, however, it was difficult for John Mitchell to defend his case. Not only did a second witness corroborate the number in the boat but some of the excursion party also gave evidence which proved the situation. The group which had hired the boat consisted of staff who worked for the Scottish Co-operative Wholesale Society and their friends. They had gone to Arnish for a picnic on Coronation Day. They each had paid a fare of 1/- [5p] for the return trip. This, it was explained, had been calculated by dividing the total cost of the boat hire by thirty-three, which meant that this had to be the number on board. These witnesses did state that they 'were not afraid of any accident when they were in the boat.'

The Procurator-Fiscal said that the charge had been proved, but attention was drawn to the wording of the charge which stated that John Mitchell 'being the owner... did proceed on an excursion.' It was pointed out that there was no evidence that John Mitchell had proceeded on the excursion; in fact the whole evidence went to show that he had not been on the boat. Finally it was decreed by the Sheriff that, 'There had been a breach of the statute, but it had been a technical offence.' The Sheriff imposed no penalty.

6. A FURTHER CLASH WITH THE TRUSTEES

In September 1942, John Mitchell applied to rent a large area of land on the opposite side of Matheson Road from his existing garage, to be used as a garage for buses – the land was 150 feet in depth and extended from Westview Terrace to what is now Macaulay Road, then described as the Barvas Road. With the shadow of the 1930s court case still looming and little friendliness between John and some of the Trustees it was no surprise that the treatment of this application did not run like clockwork.

From the start the Trustees were unwilling to grant John Mitchell his request, and a variety of reasons were put forward at their September 1942 meeting – the application letter had arrived too late for the meeting; the Town Council required to be involved; John Mitchell had other land which could be used. The size of the plan also came in for comment: 'It is on an enormous scale.'

At their next meeting, the subject was again considered, and the Trustees' opinion on the subject was divided. The discussion also became diverted from the matter in hand, with some Trustees being more concerned about the state of the existing site than the new one. 'Surely in the national interest, Mr Mitchell could transport the stuff [waste from the garage] himself to the dump where it was being collected,' was one comment. 'It was very difficult for Mr Mitchell to get anything done in the present circumstances,' said another Trustee, pointing out that some of the accommodation [presumably part of the garage buildings] had been lost due to the war. A further comment suggested that the Trustees, having complained 'more than anyone else' about John Mitchell parking his buses in front of the Porter's Lodge, on the opposite side of Bayhead Street from the garage, should do all they could to help John Mitchell achieve a tidy site. Another view was that the ground at the back of the existing garage should be tidied up first: 'Everything was higgledy piggeldy there. There was even a cement mixer out on the road.' The general feeling of the Trustees was that the present site be cleared up first, that best use then be made of it, and a proposed new site plan then be submitted. A motion supporting this was passed unanimously. There was no mention of a decision on the original request.

The Trustees were content to let the matter lie there, perhaps in the hope that no more action would be required. But John Mitchell had other ideas. In April 1943, he submitted a renewal of his application to the Trust. In this letter, he proposed the land be used as a car park and garage, stressing that, 'the need was greater than ever to enable him to meet the demand for transport in and around Stornoway.' One month later, the Trustees received an appeal against the proposal by the newly formed Lewis Association, suggesting that the area should be used for housing, that John Mitchell's proposal would worsen traffic congestion and would constitute a danger to the children resident in the then-new Manor Park housing. As they considered these matters, it was noted by the Trustees that there was no reason why the Trust should be in any hurry to grant the application as nothing could be done to develop the land while the war lasted.

On 25 June 1943, the following letter appeared in the Stornoway Gazette. Although it is anonymous, being signed simply 'Z', it does not need much imagination to guess who might have written the letter.

THE BAYHEAD GARAGE SITE

Sir, – It is encouraging to learn that people are at last getting "town-planning" conscious, but that does not of necessity mean that all else making for the well-being and convenience of the Public as a whole should be sacrificed to this end. I refer to the report of the last meeting of the Lewis Association, in your issue of June 18th, specially convened to appeal to the Stornoway Trustees to refuse a Garage site to Mr Mitchell "in an area urgently required for housing expansion." With your permission I should like to make a few comments thereon.

It strikes one as being rather curious, especially in view of the wholehearted unanimity with which the resolution was passed that, while it is the conviction of the Association, and other public bodies, that transport development is one of the first essentials for the promotion of Island prosperity, they should, at such an early stage, pass a resolution condemning this project. While it is agreed that traffic congestion is to be avoided if at all possible; is it not a fact that the building of large numbers of houses in this particular area will tend to aggravate such a condition? Whether a Garage is there or not, the same traffic problems will always be present at this junction, and on the whole is it not preferable to have a Garage here rather than abutting on the main street of the town as at present. There are but few localities in Stornoway suitable for

Mr Mitchell's purpose, whereas rather than build up the centre of the town with housing schemes there are ideal spots in the suburb for residential building.

Also it is not feasible to run a business of the nature of a Garage from widely separated localities. Is it not logical to assume that any addition to business premises must necessarily be adjacent to existing buildings? This especially applies to a Garage, which must be self-contained in the interests of efficiency and supervision. Having one building in one place and another a quarter of a mile away is impracticable.

It is also recognised that the amenities of the town should be preserved, and the erection of any building, if it conforms to the general plans of town development, should not spoil the amenities of any locality. Even a Garage can be made an attractive building if tackled with imagination and boldness.

Finally, without any doubt, the greatest requirements of Lewis as a stepping stone towards that prosperity aimed at by the Lewis Association, is an efficient transport service, both internally and externally. A very necessary adjunct to such a service and one which has been too long ignored is the provision of adequate parking spaces, for, in the absence of such facilities the traffic problems of the town will surely remain. It must be borne in mind that such spaces should be centrally situated, and if all the stationary buses, lorries, etc., at present cluttering up the streets were removed the town would wear an altogether different aspect. I have no hesitation in saying that no town of its size is so lacking in parking facilities as Stornoway, and it is regrettable that there was no constructive or useful criticism on this point by the Association at their meeting.

It is noted that the Superintendent of Police, who, I imagine, would have valuable comments to make, was not consulted before the Social Committee submitted their memorandum, and it would be interesting to get his view point on the matter, which must be of considerable concern to him. – yours etc. Z

The saga had not yet run its course. At their June 1943 meeting, the Trustees had before them a different letter from John Mitchell, asking them to reconsider his application. He wrote, 'Now that the Trustees are satisfied that the need of the people of both town and country for this accommodation [garage space] is dreadful, those who have due regard to safety and the free flow of motor traffic will certainly agree with you in granting this application.'

There is no evidence that either the contents of John Mitchell's letter or his application was discussed at any of the Trustees' meetings held during the next twelve months. It was even suggested by one Trustee that there was a deliberate attempt to 'sabotage' the application. At the January 1944 Trustees' meeting, the matter of cabbages being destroyed by sheep was considered to be of greater importance!

As a result of the prevarication of the Trustees, John Mitchell had been unable to obtain the extra space he required, and he became involved in a court case involving the parking of vehicles on Bayhead Street. In May 1944, he appeared at the Sheriff Court in Stornoway accused of 'willfully causing obstruction on the pavement and causing vehicles to stand on the public road longer than was necessary for loading or unloading goods, or picking up or setting down passengers.' Both charges were found not proven.

Undaunted, in July 1944 John Mitchell submitted alternative plans for a proposed extension of the garage on his original site at the junction of Bayhead Street and Matheson Road. The plans showed a concrete front facing the latter road, the rest of the building being in corrugated iron. At the Trustees' meeting, comment was made that there was no reference in John Mitchell's plans to the dwarf wall and railing to be erected round the Matheson Road side of the site, and that this condition, originally made in the 1930s, had never been waived by the Trustees.

Once again, some Trustees wanted to postpone their deliberations, and a decision was reached at the next meeting – though it was not the decision John Mitchell was hoping to hear, as the proposal for the extension of his garage was ruled out of order. It would seem that some of the Trustees were determined that the extension would not go ahead, in spite of one Trustee declaring, 'We are not adopting obstructionist tactics, are we?' Another added that it was, 'Mitchell, Mitchell, Mitchell,' all the time and they were beginning to get tired of it.

In addition, at the October 1944 meeting of the Trust, the members considered a new letter from John Mitchell, asking them to waive the condition in the original charter obliging him to erect a dwarf wall and railing round his garage. John's request was refused.

Eight months later, in June 1945, following a further submission from John Mitchell on his proposed extension, a final decision was made by the Stornoway Trustees. After almost three years of deliberation and prevarication, John's plan to expand his garage was unsuccessful.

The response of John Mitchell was to write a letter on the subject to the Stornoway Gazette. This appeared under the heading 'Mr Mitchell Replies,' being a 'comment on the Trustees' decision.' In his letter, John alleged that the discussion of his proposals was based not on justice but, 'personal spite, petty jealousy, and selfish personal considerations, which did not at any time take into account the needs of the community as a whole.'

He referred to the Trustees' concern regarding the local amenities and the safety of children, commenting that he had, 'noticed time and time again that the greater part of the pavement on the east side of Matheson Road, that acme of local thoroughfares, is so unfit to walk on that the children rarely use it, except the very young, who enjoy climbing on the grass verge, and the paths on top of it. There are small boulders by the dozen on the path, and pleasant walking is impossible. When rain falls, the footpath is like a relief map showing the physical features of some mountainous terrain, and streams and rivers of water flow merrily throughout its length.'

John went on to point out that children, Trustees, Town Councillors, and the ordinary man-in-the-street continue to use the road rather than the pavement, and asked, 'Can the pavement not be made usable so that the users of Matheson Road can walk in safety? Does the fact of my garage really affect road safety that much, or is it just another "road block"?'

He stated that his sole purpose in attempting to extend his garage and obtain improvements was, 'to provide more amenities of every kind for the travelling public. My garage is established at the foot of Matheson Road and there it will remain. In its present condition I am unable to say truthfully that it is satisfactory. Surely, seeing that I am established in the best spot in town, it would be of more service to the community if I was allowed to provide them with up-to-date facilities.'

In concluding, John Mitchell stated that a car belonging to one of the Trustees had twice to be sent to Glasgow for repairs, 'when, with proper foresight on the part of those concerned, it could have been possible for those repairs to have been effected locally. This is what I want to provide, an up-to-date repair depot with ample garage accommodation, and surely this would be of some benefit to the community – even to the worthy Trustees.'

7. BUS OPERATIONS DURING THE SECOND WORLD WAR

During the Second World War, John Mitchell continued to operate his buses, although wartime restrictions, especially lack of fuel, caused problems and there was some reduction in services. One of these reductions, the cutting back of the service to Ness, left the people of Eoropie, Knockaird and Fivepenny without a service. A letter in the Stornoway Gazette in January 1941 complained that, 'five hundred people are deprived of a bus, unless they walk to Lionel. Although the Ness district is only supplied with four buses for 4,000 people, we would esteem it a great favour if they arranged that one would come round these townships every morning.' The writer further complained about the unreliability of the service, complaining that, 'after travelling to Lionel in coarse weather, people have to return home as no bus at all goes to Stornoway some days. The district is suffering a lot at present, and the people are complaining very much.'

This complaint was counteracted a month later in another letter vindicating the efforts of the bus company and the drivers, stating, 'Can we not give some consideration to the diligence of these drivers in trying to overcome the difficulties they are experiencing in these trying times?... A more obliging set of owners and drivers than those on the Ness run would be difficult to find.'

Another wartime problem was the matter of soldiers having to pay their bus fares from Stornoway to their home villages when coming home on leave. The local Member of Parliament, Malcolm K Macmillan, wrote a number of letters to the War Office. In January 1941 he was able to announce that the War Office had agreed to pay bus fares for men in the Army, other than officers, although the lowest fares to townships near Stornoway would still have to come out of the soldiers' pockets. Mr Macmillan added that the Air Ministry had apologised for the delay, and it was hoped the privilege would soon extend to airmen.

The timetables published in 1943 give a good indication of the services operated by John Mitchell. Three buses each day (two on Wednesdays) operated between Ness and Stornoway, and four each day to Tolsta. Harris was served with a daily service to Rodel and one on four days each week to Leverburgh.

MITCHELL'S TRANSPORT SERVICE

CURRENT TIME TABLES.

(CUT THIS OUT FOR REFERENCE.)

Starting Point of Service:—TOWN HALL, STORNOWAY.

Terminal Points :—SANDWICK CROSS ROADS, GOATHILL, and LAXDALE (Tong Road).

TIME TABLE.

Outwards From:—	a.m.	a.m.	a.m.	a.m.	p.m.	p.m.	p.m.	p.m.	p.m.	p.m.	p.m.	p.m.	p.m.	p.m.	p.m.
TOWN HALL	9.00	10.00	11.00	12.00	1.00	2.00	3.00	4.00	5.00	6.00	7.00	8.00	9.00	10.00	11.00
SOUTH BEACH	9.00	10.00	11.00	12.00	1.00	2.00	3.00	4.00	5.00	6.00	7.00	8.00	9.00	10.00	11.00
NEWTON STREET	9.03	10.03	11.03	12.03	1.03	2.03	3.03	4.03	5.03	6.03	7.03	8.03	9.03	10.03	11.03
SEAFORTH ROAD	9.05	10.05	11.05	12.05	1.05	2.05	3.05	4.05	5.05	6.05	7.05	8.05	9.05	10.05	11.05
SANDWICK PARK	9.08	10.08	11.08	12.08	1.08	2.08	3.08	4.08	5.08	6.08	7.08	8.08	9.08	10.08	11.08
SANDWICK CROSS ROADS	9.10	10.10	11.10	12.10	1.10	2.10	3.10	4.10	5.10	6.10	7.10	8.10	9.10	10.10	11.10
SANDWICK CROSS ROADS	9.10	10.10	11.10	12.10	1.10	2.10	3.10	4.10	5.10	6.10	7.10	8.10	9.10	10.10	11.10
SANDWICK PARK	9.12	10.12	11.12	12.12	1.12	2.12	3.12	4.12	5.12	6.12	7.12	8.12	9.12	10.12	11.12
SEAFORTH ROAD	9.15	10.15	11.15	12.15	1.15	2.15	3.15	4.15	5.15	6.15	7.15	8.15	9.15	10.15	11.15
NEWTON STREET	9.17	10.17	11.17	12.17	1.17	2.17	3.17	4.17	5.17	6.17	7.17	8.17	9.17	10.17	11.17
SOUTH BEACH	9.19	10.19	11.19	12.19	1.19	2.19	3.19	4.19	5.19	6.19	7.19	8.19	9.19	10.19	11.19
TOWN HALL	9.19	10.19	11.19	12.19	1.19	2.19	3.19	4.19	5.19	6.19	7.19	8.19	9.19	10.19	11.19
PERCIVAL SQUARE	9.20	10.20	11.20	12.20	1.20	2.20	3.20	4.20	5.20	6.20	7.20	8.20	9.20	10.20	
CHURCH STREET	9.22	10.22	11.22	12.22	1.22	2.22	3.22	4.22	5.22	6.22	7.22	8.22	9.22	10.22	
HOSPITAL	9.25	10.25	11.25	12.25	1.25	2.25	3.25	4.25	5.25	6.25	7.25	8.25	9.25	10.25	
FOOTBALL FIELD	9.27	10.27	11.27	12.27	1.27	2.27	3.27	4.27	5.27	6.27	7.27	8.27	9.27	10.27	
GOATHILL FARM	9.29	10.29	11.29	12.29	1.29	2.29	3.29	4.29	5.29	6.29	7.29	8.29	9.29	10.29	
GOATHILL FARM	9.30	10.30	11.30	12.30	1.30	2.30	3.30	4.30	5.30	6.30	7.30	8.30	9.30	10.30	
FOOTBALL FIELD	9.32	10.32	11.32	12.32	1.32	2.32	3.32	4.32	5.32	6.32	7.32	8.32	9.32	10.32	
HOSPITAL	9.34	10.34	11.34	12.34	1.34	2.34	3.34	4.34	5.34	6.34	7.34	8.34	9.34	10.34	
CHURCH STREET	9.38	10.38	11.38	12.38	1.38	2.38	3.38	4.38	5.38	6.38	7.38	8.38	9.38	10.38	
CROMWELL STREET	9.40	10.40	11.40	12.40	1.40	2.40	3.40	4.40	5.40	6.40	7.40	8.40	9.40	10.40	
CHURCH STREET CORNER	9.40	10.40	11.40	12.40	1.40	2.40	3.40	4.40	5.40	6.40	7.40	8.40	9.40	10.40	
STAG ROAD CORNER	9.43	10.43	11.43	12.43	1.43	2.43	3.43	4.43	5.43	6.43	7.43	8.43	9.43	10.43	
COULREGREIN CORNER	9.45	10.45	11.45	12.45	1.45	2.45	3.45	4.45	5.45	6.45	7.45	8.45	9.45	10.45	
LAXDALE CROSS ROADS	9.47	10.47	11.47	12.47	1.47	2.47	3.47	4.47	5.47	6.47	7.47	8.47	9.47	10.47	
LAXDALE TONG ROAD	9.49	10.49	11.49	12.49	1.49	2.49	3.49	4.49	5.49	6.49	7.49	8.49	9.49	10.49	
LAXDALE TONG ROAD	9.50	10.50	11.50	12.50	1.50	2.50	3.50	4.50	5.50	6.50	7.50	8.50	9.50	10.50	
LAXDALE CROSS ROAD	9.52	10.52	11.52	12.52	1.52	2.52	3.52	4.52	5.52	6.52	7.52	8.52	9.52	10.52	
COULREGREIN ROAD	9.54	10.54	11.54	12.54	1.54	2.54	3.54	4.54	5.54	6.54	7.54	8.54	9.54	10.54	
STAG ROAD	9.57	10.57	11.57	12.57	1.57	2.57	3.57	4.57	5.57	6.57	7.57	8.57	9.57	10.57	
PERCIVAL SQUARE	9.59	10.59	11.59	12.59	1.59	2.59	3.59	4.59	5.59	6.59	7.59	8.59	9.59	10.59	

TIME-TABLE.   MELBOST—STORNOWAY.

FRIDAY.					SATURDAY.			
Leave Stornoway	1.00 p.m.	Arrive Melbost	1.15 p.m.		Leave Stornoway	2.00 p.m.	Arrive Melbost	2.15 p.m.
Town Hall	5.00 p.m.		5.15 p.m.		Town Hall	5.30 p.m.		5.45 p.m.
						9.30 p.m.		9.45 p.m.
					Leave Melbost	2.30 p.m.	Arrive Stornoway	2.45 p.m.
Leave Melbost	1.30 p.m.	Arrive Stornoway	1.45 p.m.			6.00 p.m.		6.15 p.m.
	5.30 p.m.		5.45 p.m.			10.00 p.m.		10.15 p.m.

Copies of this Time-Table can be obtained from Mitchell's Garage—Price 1d.

Above and overleaf: Timetable of the services operated in 1943.

MITCHELL'S TRANSPORT SERVICE

CURRENT TIME TABLES.

(CUT THIS OUT FOR REFERENCE.)

NESS — STORNOWAY.

DAILY EXCEPT WEDNESDAY AND SUNDAY.

Leave PORT OF NESS	9.00 a.m.	2.00 p.m.	6.00 p.m.
SWAINBOST	9.08 a.m.	2.08 p.m.	6.08 p.m.
CROSS	9.13 a.m.	2.13 p.m.	6.13 p.m.
DELL	9.17 a.m.	2.17 p.m.	6.17 p.m.
GALSON	9.27 a.m.	2.27 p.m.	6.27 p.m.
BORVE	9.35 a.m.	2.35 p.m.	6.35 p.m.
SHADER	9.40 a.m.	2.40 p.m.	6.40 p.m.
BARVAS	9.55 a.m.	2.55 p.m.	6.55 p.m.
LAXDALE	10.20 a.m.	3.20 p.m.	6.20 p.m.
STORNOWAY	10.25 a.m.	3.25 p.m.	6.25 p.m.

Leave STORNOWAY	12.30 p.m.	6.30 p.m.	
LAXDALE	12.35 p.m.	6.35 p.m.	15
BARVAS	12.55 p.m.	6.55 p.m.	minutes
SHADER	1.10 p.m.	7.10 p.m.	after
BORVE	1.15 p.m.	7.15 p.m.	the
GALSON	1.23 p.m.	7.23 p.m.	arrival
DELL	1.33 p.m.	7.33 p.m.	of
CROSS	1.38 p.m.	7.38 p.m.	mailboat
SWAINBOST	1.45 p.m.	7.45 p.m.	
PORT-OF-NESS	1.55 p.m.	7.55 p.m.	

WEDNESDAYS.

Leave PORT-OF-NESS	9.00 a.m.	6.00 p.m.
Leave STORNOWAY	2.00 p.m.	15 minutes after arrival of boat

STORNOWAY — TOLSTA.

DAILY EXCEPT SUNDAYS.

Ex STORNOWAY	11.20 a.m.	3.20 p.m.	6.20 p.m.	
LAXDALE	11.26 a.m.	3.26 p.m.	6.26 p.m.	15 Minutes
TONG	11.35 a.m.	3.35 p.m.	6.35 p.m.	after the
COLL	11.43 a.m.	3.43 p.m.	6.43 p.m.	arrival
BACK	11.45 a.m.	3.45 p.m.	6.45 p.m.	of
GRESS	11.52 a.m.	3.52 p.m.	6.52 p.m.	Mailboat
TOLSTA	12. 6 p.m.	4. 6 p.m.	7. 6 p.m.	

Ex TOLSTA	9.20 a.m.	12.20 p.m.	4.20 p.m.	7.20 p.m.
GRESS	9.34 a.m.	12.34 p.m.	4.34 p.m.	7.34 p.m.
BACK	9.41 a.m.	12.41 p.m.	4.41 p.m.	7.41 p.m.
COLL	9.43 a.m.	12.43 p.m.	4.43 p.m.	7.43 p.m.
TONG	9.50 a.m.	12.50 p.m.	4.50 p.m.	7.50 p.m.
LAXDALE	9.59 a.m.	12.59 p.m.	4.59 p.m.	7.59 p.m.

LEVERBURGH — STORNOWAY.

Via FINSBAY and GEOCRAB ON MONDAY, THURSDAY and SATURDAY.
Via BORVE ON MONDAY and FRIDAY.

Leave LEVERBURGH	8.30 a.m.	Leave STORNOWAY		6.30 p.m.
TARBERT	10.15 a.m.	BALALLAN		7.00 p.m.
ARIVRUAICH	11.15 a.m.	ARIVRUAICH		7.15 p.m.
BALALLAN	11.25 a.m.	TARBERT		8.15 p.m.
Arrive STORNOWAY	12.00 noon	Arrive LEVERBURGH		10.00 p.m.

SATURDAY ONLY.

Leave LEVERBURGH	8.30 a.m.	Leave STORNOWAY	9.30 p.m.

STORNOWAY to RODEL

(Via Borve).

TUESDAY, THURSDAY, SATURDAY.

	Time.	
Leave	9.30 a.m.	Stornoway
	9.52 a.m.	Soval
	10.3 a.m.	Laxay
	10.9 a.m.	Balallan
	10.20 a.m.	Arivruach
	10.42 a.m.	Ardvourlie
	10.51 a.m.	Marig
	11.30 a.m.	Tarbert
	11.43 a.m.	Grosebay
	12.2 p.m.	Laxdale
	12.22 p.m.	Borve Lodge
	12.36 p.m.	Scarastabeg
	12.41 p.m.	Northton
	12.49 p.m.	Leverburgh
	1.0 p.m.	Rodel

RODEL to STORNOWAY

(Via Geocrab).

TUESDAY, THURSDAY, SATURDAY.

	Time.	
Leave	3.00 p.m.	Rodel
	3.24 p.m.	Finsbay
	3.32 p.m.	Flodibay
	3.40 p.m.	Manish
	3.49 p.m.	Geocrab
	3.57 p.m.	Lacklee
	4.05 p.m.	Grosebay
	5.30 p.m.	Tarbert
	5.53 p.m.	Marig
	6.04 p.m.	Ardvourlie
	6.30 p.m.	Arivruach
	6.42 p.m.	Balallan
	6.48 p.m.	Laxay
	7.00 p.m.	Soval
Arrive	7.30 p.m.	Stornoway

STORNOWAY to RODEL

(Via Geocrab).

MONDAY, WEDNESDAY, FRIDAY.

	Time.	
Leave	9.30 a.m.	Stornoway
	9.50 a.m.	Soval
	10.02 a.m.	Laxay
	10.12 a.m.	Balallan
	10.30 a.m.	Arivruach
	10.50 a.m.	Ardvourlie
	11.05 a.m.	Marig
	11.30 a.m.	Tarbert
	11.45 a.m.	Grosebay
	11.50 a.m.	Lacklee
	12.01 p.m.	Geocrab
	12.10 p.m.	Manish
	12.18 p.m.	Flodibay
	12.36 p.m.	Finsbay
	12.50 p.m.	Rodel

RODEL to STORNOWAY

(Via Borve).

MONDAY, WEDNESDAY, FRIDAY.

	Time.	
Leave	3.00 p.m.	Rodel
	3.09 p.m.	Leverburgh
	3.15 p.m.	Northton
	3.19 p.m.	Scarastabeg
	3.30 p.m.	Borve Lodge
	3.45 p.m.	Laxdale
	4.05 p.m.	Grosebay
	5.30 p.m.	Tarbert
	5.53 p.m.	Marig
	6.04 p.m.	Ardvourlie
	6.30 p.m.	Arivruach
	6.42 p.m.	Balallan
	6.48 p.m.	Laxay
	7.00 p.m.	Soval
Arrive	7.30 p.m.	Stornoway

ALL THE ABOVE SERVICES ARE FROM THE TRANSPORT OFFICE, CROMWELL STREET.

The town service operated hourly from 9am until 11pm. Its route was from the Town Hall via Newton to Sandwick and return, followed by a journey up Church Street to Goathill Farm. On return from there a journey was made as far as Tong Road at Laxdale. These three journeys were timetabled to take fifty-nine minutes, thus leaving one minute before the next circuit commenced. In addition two afternoon services on Fridays and three on Saturdays were provided to Melbost. There were, of course, no buses operating anywhere on Sundays.

John Mitchell was also involved in organising the transport of workers to the airport during the war, although this service would appear not to have been operated with a set timetable; it must be assumed that buses ran when they were required.

Although accidents were few and far between, in 1943 Mitchell's buses were involved in three accidents. The first took place on Oliver's Brae, and involved a cyclist who swerved from the side of the road and came into contact with a bus. The injured cyclist was taken to hospital but sadly died from his injuries the following morning. The second accident proved to be less severe. A ten-year-old boy fell from one of the buses and received serious head injuries. The Gazette reported he was 'understood to have fallen from the emergency door at the rear of the bus.'

Later in March one of John Mitchell's drivers appeared in court charged with careless driving, after being involved in a collision with a lorry at the junction of Matheson Road and Church Street.

The lorry ran on for twenty-eight feet beyond the point of impact and then overturned. The bus was the more extensively damaged. The right front spring was twisted back and almost split, although it was made of solid steel. The rear part of the spring punctured the sump. The steering column was so badly twisted to be beyond repair. The total damage to the bus was estimated to be approximately £400.

An eye witness account said both vehicles sounded their horns, the lorry crossed the junction travelling 'pretty fast' while the bus slowed down but speeded up again as it reached the junction. Passengers on the bus said that 'They were not even jolted by the impact,' a somewhat contradictory statement, given what had happened. More confusing evidence followed. The lorry driver said in his defence that as soon as he noticed the bus he realised it was no use trying to stop, adding, 'The bus would have got in front of the lorry. The first thing the driver of the bus said to me was that he had no means of stopping. I took it from that that his brakes were defective.' John Mitchell said the vehicles were travelling at right angles to each other. The right

Stornoway Gazette 25 December 1942

IT WASN'T A JOY RIDE

A number of John Mitchell's drivers did not stay in Stornoway, but had homes at the end of a country route. It was the custom for them to keep their bus overnight at the end of the last service. As there were no Sunday services, buses would remain at the driver's house until the first service on the following Monday morning. On this occasion the bus was spotted in Stornoway long after the departure of the last bus, leading to questions being asked and the ensuing complex court case.

The question whether one of Mitchell's buses was taken from Tolsta to Stornoway on Saturday night, 5th December, for repairs, or whether the driver came to town for a jaunt, was investigated at some length when Donald Maciver, 28 North Tolsta, appeared before Sheriff Smart, on Friday, charged with (1) Being in charge of a bus while under the influence of drink; (2) Taking it without the owner's consent; (3) Making a journey for which there was no insurance in force; (4) Using petrol for an unauthorized purpose; and (5) Failing to immobilize the bus.

Sheriff Smart found him guilty on the first charge, fined him £10 and disqualified him from driving for twelve months. He also found him guilty on the fifth charge and admonished him.

He found the three other charges not proven.

The police said in evidence that Maciver's bus should not have been in town at the time they found it on North Beach quay, because the last run for the day had been made, and the bus was garaged at Tolsta.

Maciver's explanation was that on the way to Tolsta he had trouble with the clutch and steering gear. It would not have been safe to use the bus on Monday morning with a full load of passengers, so he went back to town to have it repaired. He had been at work from 7.30am and had only half an hour for lunch. He was sorely in need of some thing (sic) to eat and didn't feel like walking down town from the garage, so he took the bus as far as North Beach quay, meaning to go to his sister's for a cup of tea. His sister's house was locked, and he fell in with a pal home on leave with whom he had two nips of rum and two half-pints of beer.

Called as a witness for the prosecution, Mr Mitchell said he knew of no reason why the bus should have been in Stornoway at that time on Saturday night.

The Fiscal – Do you not agree that this was just a joy ride? – It hasn't developed into a joy ride anyway.

Cross-examined by Mr J D Scoular, solicitor, defending, Mr Mitchell agreed that the bus had been ditched a few days earlier because of trouble with the steering gear, and that it had been in the garage again for repairs a day or two after 5th December.

The Fiscal – Did you tell the police that you wanted to deal with this irregular use of your buses? – I don't know whether I should really answer that question.

Angus Allan Morrison, one of the passengers in Maciver's bus on the last run to Tolsta, said he heard the driver tell the passengers that he would not go with the bus again till it had been repaired again.

Dr R M Fraser certified that Maciver was under the influence of drink and the same view was expressed by Sergt. Macphail, Constable John Mackenzie, Back, and Constable J K Macdonald.

"Under the influence of drink is a very elastic term," said Sheriff Smart to Constable Mackenzie. "In plain language, was he drunk?" "Yes," replied the constable. "Visibly drunk?" asked the Sheriff. "Yes," replied the constable.

Sheriff Smart said he was not at all satisfied on the question whether the journey was made with the implied consent of the owner, and the other two charges relating to the validity of the insurance and the use of petrol hinged on that point.

chassis frame of the bus was extensively damaged. The left chassis frame was not damaged at all, which was a clear indication that the bus was at a standstill at the moment of impact. The lorry must have swerved across in front of it. The driver was fined three pounds (with the option of twenty days), although the Sheriff said the major part of the blame rested with the other driver.

Severe weather played havoc with the bus services on a number of occasions during the war years. In January 1941 after a week of steady snowfall a gale sprang up and the snow quickly began to drift. In a little over an hour every main road on the island became blocked. This led to a number of problems for Mitchell's buses and their passengers, some of whom made heroic efforts to reach their destinations.

When a Harris bus broke down in the snow a man from Scalpay tramped almost forty miles through wind and snow to attend his wedding at Gress. A second bus from Harris became stranded in a drift between Ardhasaig and the Clisham. The bus had left Tarbert at 6 pm and eventually the driver and his passengers gave up the struggle at Maaruig about nine o'clock. Some spent the night there, while the driver walked with another passenger about four miles to Ardvourlie, where they spent the night. They arrived there exhausted, their clothes frozen and packed with snow which had blown under their coats. The following day the driver managed to reach Balallan Post Office, from where he contacted the garage in Stornoway. They were told that John Mitchell had left town with a car to pick them up so they started walking to meet the car. They eventually reached Stornoway without seeing any sign of John and his car. He had tried to reach them by another road which was also blocked. The bus had also been carrying mail, bound for Stornoway and then onward by the mail steamer to the mainland. It was arranged to take the mail back to Tarbert, to be conveyed by the ordinary steamer service from there.

One of the biggest drifts was at Oliver's Brae, just outside Stornoway. At 9 o'clock one evening one of Mitchell's buses passed without difficulty. Only half-an-hour later the road had become almost impassable and soon there was a string of ten buses and cars stranded in the drift. Most of the buses had full loads of workers travelling home to Point, so there were almost 200 willing pairs of hands pushing and heaving to get the vehicles through the snow.

Another experience during this time of snowdrifts and road blockages involved John Mitchell's buses and a policeman returning home from Stornoway to Back. He was on the last bus from town, which, because of the snow, only managed to reach Laxdale, a couple of miles outside town. The policeman, determined to reach home, decided to walk on from there. He reached Tong, where he came on an assortment of vehicles, including another of Mitchell's buses, stuck in a drift. The policeman helped others with the pushing and pulling and finally they managed to get the bus clear. The driver assumed that the policeman was travelling in one of the other vehicles and drove off, leaving the policeman standing in the snow. He had to finish his journey on foot, finally reaching Back at quarter past two in the morning. The bus later became stranded in a drift at Gress, and spent the night there.

The next spell of bad weather was January 1945. During the third week of the month there was heavy snowfall on the Thursday, but traffic was not seriously disrupted except to Uig. A bus became stranded at Achmore, and the driver and passengers were forced to spend the night there. The bus was still there the following Monday.

More snow on Saturday of that week caused more problems. The mail-boat buses, which would wait until the mail boat from the mainland had arrived in the evening, were unable to go to Point, Back, South Lochs or Uig. The police, anticipating the situation, contacted the hotels in Stornoway to enable passengers arriving off the steamer to remain in town, although it was not until after midnight that the *Lochness* finally arrived.

John Mitchell wisely cancelled the bus for Tarbert on the Saturday afternoon. John instead used his shooting brake (his own estate car) to take three passengers for Harris. They were encouraged by the report that a lorry load of men had left Tarbert to clear the drifts on the Clisham. Just past Aridhbhruaich the travellers encountered a mile-long snow drift and the driver decided to return to Stornoway. The passengers decided to continue on foot, reaching only as far as Ardvourlie, some seven miles further on, after struggling for about four hours through deep snow and several snow showers. Staying there overnight they finally reached their destination on Sunday afternoon. The shooting brake fared little better, becoming stuck on its return trip.

8. MEMORIES: DONALD MACLEOD (DÒMHNALL BHOBSAIDH)

Life in the garage and on the buses during the Second World War

I started work in Mitchell's garage as an apprentice motor mechanic in 1943. The pay was fifteen shillings a week, but I was getting the bus up and down (from home at Gress) to work for nothing and then going up town every night for nothing. Looking back on these old times you realise how far the world has moved on.

At the time John Mitchell's bus service covered most of the island. He also had contracts for conveying workers to the aerodrome, where a great deal of civil engineering work was going on. He had enormous problems: there were very few drivers available on the island at the time. Only doctors and business people owned cars, and the lads who were able to drive were in the forces. Most of the buses were 'past their sell by date', had seen better days with Alexanders and SMT (major bus companies on the mainland). It took a laid-back character like John to 'keep the show on the road'. He could take anything in his stride and deal with any difficulty with a witty retort.

For us young lads in the garage the main objective was to learn to drive. As soon as John went home for his dinner we were out on the road, doing a circular tour 'Matheson Road and Stag Road' with any vehicle that was available. If he came back early we were in trouble, we were severely reprimanded. Thinking about these dressing-downs I realised it was only a bit of kidology on John's part. He knew we were doing the 'Stag run', as we called it, and the sooner we learnt to drive the more useful we became to him. Age didn't seem to matter a lot. This became clear to me, as shortly after one of the rows, 'given the red card' and banned from all vehicles, he came up to me and asked, 'Do you think you could manage to do a hire to Point? Take the Vauxhall 12 out on the road so you can get used to the gears.' Though my driving ability would be regarded as questionable, the only snag that came to mind was finding my way to Point. I knew where Point was, but the road layout beyond Newton was new to me. John sorted that problem. 'There is a Henderson car (another motor hirer) involved as well, it will be parked outside the County Hotel, you just follow him.'

After completing my DIY driving test, I parked behind Henderson's car. After a short wait, Malcolm Macmillan (the local MP at the time) and three important looking characters from Westminster came out of the hotel. John Mitchell had never told me what the hire was for. It was about the Portnaguran pier, a meeting was being held about the pier. Macmillan and one of the men got in the front car and the other two into mine.

Now everybody who drives will agree that hill starts can be a bit tricky during the learning period. Having two government officials in the back seat makes the exercise slightly more demanding. I was parked on the steepest hill I had encountered in my short driving career. I'd never started on a hill before, but after a lot of struggle we got away. By the time I got going the other car had disappeared, so the second problem arose: finding my way to Portnaguran (no road or village signs in those days). The dodgy start to the journey certainly quietened the two talkative gentlemen in the back. My memory fails me concerning the rest of the drive except for the amount of peat on the road. The Point folk were taking their peats home, and my amateurish swerving about dodging peats (which would have fallen from carts) must have had the two lads in the back wishing they had never left London. Though at the time Hitler was trying his best to bomb the place out of existence I am sure they would have felt safer there.

While on the subject of dodgy driving, one of the tasks we had to perform quite often was digging buses out of peat. The Lochs moor, especially, tended to drag them off the road. The excuse always was 'swerving to avoid sheep or fog'. I'm sure that John didn't fall for that one, but what could he do? We spent some pleasant days on the Lochs moor armed with jacks and planks of timber. The buses had to be returned to the road the hard way. There were no mobile cranes or recovery machines on the island at the time. John himself used to be in charge of these outings and I'm sure that he always enjoyed himself; he was always in a good mood on these occasions.

There was a bus running to Harris at six o'clock; it went as far as Rodel and came back the next morning. The driver of this bus approached me one day in the garage, requesting: would I do the run for him for a week as he was desperate to get some time off? I thought he was joking, and said, 'What would Mitchell say about that?' Considering my age and limited driving experience, I didn't think for a moment that John was going to give his consent. Off he went and soon returned telling me that Mitchell said it would be OK. I was amazed! Mitchell never came to me and never said anything at all. The driver's next question was: would I come along with him right away. This was at

John surveys the damage to one of his buses after it had run into a ditch.
The bus had suffered damage to the front wheel and windows had been broken.

three o'clock in the afternoon and the bus was going at six. When
he saw that I was a bit hesitant (wondering how it would be possible
to get home), he said that he would give me an old motorbike. There
was another snag: it wasn't possible to let them know at home that I
wouldn't be arriving from work that night. In those days there was no
telephone. The Harris run went reasonably well, although they were
not too pleased at home with me doing that kind of work at my age.
I was only sixteen, and I had no licence.

There was another time the windows fell in. It was the same week
that I went over to Harris. The driver he lived in Airidhbhruaich; he
came in to town with me that day and it was obvious he was drinking
all day. He was a jolly sort of a character and going home he said, 'I'll
take the bus, I'll drive it, as far as my own house. So off we went and
we had just reached the Marybank road when one of Tawse's lorries –
they were building the airport at the time – when part of the tailboard
caught the bus and knocked the windows, blew the windows in. He
kept going, but I told him to stop. There was a bit of a bend in the road,
and by the time he had stopped we couldn't see the lorry, and when we
went back it had gone. We carried on and got down to Tarbert, I let the
other driver off at his own house. At Tarbert there was a police station
there. A policeman appeared, saying, 'Did you have an accident?'
I said, 'No.' he looked at the bus and saw there were no windows.

'How did this happen?' 'It was when I was backing out of the garage.' But it was no good telling lies because the driver of the lorry reported it to the police station in Stornoway and they had phoned to Tarbert.

At the court case Colin Scott Mackenzie was the sheriff and a lot of the passengers who were in the bus were there as witnesses and they were all on the driver's side. And there was this fellow, he was 'a bit slow' and they asked him, 'What did you think when you saw the glass in the windows coming in?' Oh, he didn't think anything of it. 'Do the windows always fall in on top of you?'

Another time, doing a relief stint on the Lemreway run, the bus departed North Beach at 6.30 but adhering to the timetable wasn't always that easy. It would seem that all the passengers who came into town on the bus had to be accounted for going home. There were three men missing this day I started on the run. I was told they would be in the Royal (Hotel). I parked outside the hotel and went inside to get them out. They were there all right and suddenly a pint was stuck in my hand. Well, I thought, might as well have a swig seeing it's there. Next thing a huge hand dropped on my shoulder, the unmistakable voice behind me bellowing, 'What are you doing in here?' Yes, John had problems moving passengers round the island, one way or another. He never mentioned the incident to me again. That's the sort of person he was, taking everything in his stride, and taking more chances than anybody I have ever met.

Another time I had the job of taking workers to the aerodrome in the mornings on my way to work. Some of the buses used on that job could be classed as 'a bit ropey.' We had one with no sides, a relic from the 'Golden Mile', Blackpool, I expect. With a bit of modification it carried out the aerodrome duties. With some of the old Albions the only means of starting the engine was by a starting-handle, a permanent fixture in the front. Starting these old engines up on a cold, wet morning could be quite demanding, and it was important to be on time. If they arrive late, so losing money, there was pandemonium. To keep things running smoothly, I found the best starting method was to park the bus overnight on the Tolsta road above Gress. 'Beinn Iomhair' (the local name for the steep hill) did the trick every time. On another occasion I started taking the Gress folk to church on Sundays. Carrying out this task resulted in me being 'pounced on from a great height' by a lady from Back: 'for breaking the Sabbath'.

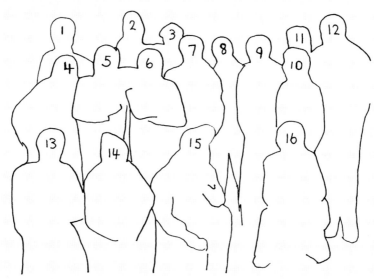

Mitchell's Garage staff in 1946.
As was the case throughout the island, most people were known by their nicknames.
1. Ivor Mackay (Tolsta) 2. Willie Logan 3. Neil Mitchell 4. Donald Melbost
5. Ivor Macleod (an Coilean) 6. Dòmhnall Geal (Newmarket) 7. Donald Macleod
(Dòmhnall Bhobsaidh) 8. Not known 9. Iain Nis 10. Toovie Morrison 11. Donny Murray
12. John Murray (Iain Mòr) 13. Aonghas an Ach 14. Dave Macfarlane 15. Not known
16. Not known

Keeping the old buses running and private car repairs kept us busy in the garage. Obtaining spare parts was a problem, so more components had to be repaired than what happens at the present time. Due to the poor quality wartime oil and petrol available, burnt valves, bearing and excessive cylinder wear was frequent.

The garage was very cold in the winter time. We had central heating: a fire in the middle of the floor. Not the 'taigh dubh' (black house) style but a brazier of glowing coke. I don't think the health and safety officials and insurance assessors would regard our heating arrangements as very appropriate for a garage. You couldn't disagree with them, as buckets of petrol on the floor was our means of washing greasy components! Yes, we had a few fires going. We didn't need any help from the Luftwaffe to put the fire-buckets to use. We must have been half decent fire-fighters, as the garage survived.

At the age of eighteen I was conscripted and got my trade in the army as a vehicle mechanic. A six-month course in Aldershot came in very useful, as I'm afraid the theory side of the game was a bit 'thin on the ground' in the garage. No day-release to college in those days.

On returning to the garage I found everything greatly improved. Plenty of drivers available, and as the driving and PSV tests had been reintroduced (all tests were suspended during the war years) the standard of driving was at a much higher level. The bus fleet had also advanced. Some new utility model Bedfords had been introduced. The yearly testing of buses kept them in a good, roadworthy condition.

9. THE DEATH OF JOHN MITCHELL'S FATHER

A sad event for the Mitchell family occurred when George Mitchell, John's father, passed away on 14 March 1945. While he was never directly connected with any of John's businesses, he was, as his obituary below clearly shows, a strong character who would have had immense bearing on John's upbringing and attitude to life. He became ill while in Stornoway on business and was taken to the Lewis Hospital in Stornoway where after two operations he died a few days later. Not many had known that he had poor health during the previous few years, as, typical of the man, he had not complained.

Having been a fisherman it was not surprising that he had joined the Royal Naval Reserve, and when the First World War broke out he was selected to join the Lewis Coastal Patrol. While on this service he acquitted himself with such courage and distinction that when his ship was in harbour he was especially exempt from all shore duties.

After the end of the First World War, George became a familiar figure on the West Side as 'roadman' for the stretch between Dalbeg and Bragar, tackling the job with 'characteristic skill and energy.' A fitting tribute to him appeared in the Stornoway Gazette, which is reproduced here.

Overleaf: John Mitchell owned this bus, a Bedford with a Duple body, between 1944 and the early 1960s. It is seen here operating on the Harris service.

When the ripe ear falls to the reaper's scythe, when the old lay down their burdens, and the struggle for existence ends, when Nature fulfils her laws in the orderly manner we expect of Nature, mankind take but little notice but, occasionally in our sequestered vale, Nature gives a jolt as if to remind us of our insignificance and impotence. Such a shock was given to the village of Shawbost last week by the news of the death in the Lewis Hospital of one of its most popular citizens – George Mitchell. Only the Friday before, in the full figure of lusty manhood, had he gone to town on business. There he was taken suddenly ill. He underwent an operation on Saturday, and though reports of his condition were unfavourable, it was difficult to believe that George would not appear among us hale and hearty once again. But it was not to be. Fate had decreed that his work on earth was ended – work, in whichever sphere he laboured, he performed with exceptional skill and deftness of hand. George Mitchell was one of nature's gentlemen. He exuded gentleness in such a way that even the atmosphere in which he moved seemed permeated to such an extent that it was impossible for any other thought to enter but that of rectitude and purity. The largest concourse of people, probably the largest ever seen in Shawbost, which followed his remains to Dalmore Cemetery on Saturday last, testified to the very great esteem in which he was held by the whole of the West Side. George was one of those silent, strong men whose strength of character gives a distinctly high tone to their place of residence, and whose departure creates a blank in the lives of all who knew him. "A' chuid de Pharos da" [May he have his share of paradise].

10. POST-WAR DEVELOPMENTS AND DIFFICULTIES

The end of the Second World War may have seen a return to peace on Lewis, but conditions were far from what they had been prior to 1939. Austerity was the order of the day, machines and vehicles had become overused and worn out, and spare parts were hard to come by. In addition, the island roads, never of a high standard to begin with, had suffered from years of poor and lack of maintenance.

The importance of the services provided by John Mitchell and some of the difficulties involved with running the business, were aptly described in an article written by Ashley Taylor which appeared in 'The Commercial Motor' in January 1950. It was entitled 'Buses Improve living in the Hebrides.'

> The Mitchell organization now covers the full length and breadth of the island, some 70 miles by 25, with the exception of six miles in one direction. To give this coverage, the vehicles have to traverse many rough roads and at least half of the mileage is over untarred surfaces, the track width in the majority of cases being under 10 ft., with periodic 'loops' to allow vehicles travelling in opposite directions to pass each other.

> To deal with these conditions, straightforward stage-carriage bodywork is required, and those who know the state of the roads will not be surprised to learn that every machine in the fleet has suffered damage because of the rough surfaces.

> Apart from body repairs, spring breakages on one or other of the vehicles are liable to be weekly occurrences. Those who know the island well tell me that there is under 15 miles of highway which the mainland operator would regard as passably good. Some of the highways may be likened to motor trials sections, and Mr. Mitchell informed me that on several occasions it has been necessary to send out rescue parties to buses which while stationary had sunk into the ground.

> All the Mitchell services are run to and from Stornoway, three machines, which cover 130 miles a day each, running on routes

to the extremities of Lewis. Three more vehicles operate a 32-mile route from Stornoway, whilst others are on a 35-mile run and one works a 50-mile circuit: in addition, there are town operations and a 15-mile route which is given 10 runs daily.

By this means the scattered communities of Lewis and Harris are connected together, being provided with newspapers and many necessities by means of the parcels service. Many consignments of Harris Tweed, which is made in both the islands, are transported. Mails are also carried on the Harris route.

For obvious reasons, passenger fares are higher than is usual on the mainland, but no one could justifiably grumble in view of the operating difficulties involved. For fares collection Setright machines have been used on country runs since before the war, whilst the T.I.M. system is employed on town routes.

In summertime the Mitchell fleet ran day and half-day tours to the various places of interest in the island, such as Rodel, Ness, North Tolsta, Callanish and Uig. Evening trips are a popular feature with both visitors and the local inhabitants.

The fleet owner in Lewis has every incentive to carry out all possible maintenance and overhaul work within his own organization for, apart from running costs, the freight charges for taking a vehicle to specialists of any kind on the mainland, are considerable, even the lightest buses costing over £20 for the single journey by sea from Stornoway.

In view of the arduous conditions with which vehicles have to cope, it is impossible to have a set mileage system for overhauls, as even on a new vehicle spring renewals may be needed during the first week. Thus a system of constant inspection and running maintenance, is employed.

Until a quarter of a century ago the situation of many of the villagers in these Western Isles was inexpressibly remote, but with the development of road transport matters improved, and with the coming of the scheduled services residents in many a tiny scattered community are now in reach of modern life.'

It was under these conditions that John Mitchell set about restoring and improving his bus services. In 1945 he submitted an application to the Traffic Commissioners to operate a daily circular service round the West Side [the route serving Callanish, Carloway and Barvas], but this was put into 'cold storage' because it had appeared too late to give the other operators time to consider it. When the Commissioners returned to Stornoway in May 1946, the postponed application for the service was heard and approved. The service was quickly put into operation, with an anticlockwise run leaving Stornoway at 3pm and a clockwise one departing at 9.30pm.

Early in 1947 Mr Mitchell added yet another service, to Leurbost, Crossbost, Ranish and Grimshader. He took over the North Lochs services of Donald Macleod of Leurbost and Donald Mackenzie of Crossbost, who had both indicated they no longer wished to operate their service. It was clear to all parties that there was insufficient traffic for two operators, and accordingly it was agreed with the Traffic Commissioners that the service would be shared between John Mitchell and Lochs Motor Transport Ltd.

An argument over the Melbost service

In May 1947, an application had been made by Hebridean Transport Ltd to operate a service to the Braighe. This was at the other end of a beach, a few miles from Stornoway, and to which the people of the town would often go for picnics. It was about a mile from John Mitchell's terminus at Melbost. John Mitchell opposed the application, stating that he had runs from Stornoway to Melbost every day up to eleven o'clock at night and he had heard no great outcry from the people of Stornoway for access to the beach apart from the service which he provided.

John Mitchell was of the opinion that he had a monopoly to run from Stornoway to Melbost (this was definitely not the case, although it may have been John's own opinion on the matter), and that he considered that there was no sense in the proposal for a new service as it would just land Hebridean Transport Ltd in unnecessary expense. Further argument, at times verging on farcical, then followed. When Hebridean Transport Ltd's solicitor returned to the question of an alleged monopoly, John Mitchell declined to answer as he had already answered it. 'You can ask as long as you like,' he said. 'I can sit here as long as you can stand.' The solicitor then argued that Mitchell's service to Melbost did not serve people wanting to go to the beach at the Braighe. John Mitchell responded by saying that his service took people within a stone's throw of the beach on both sides of the isthmus.

'How far can you throw a stone?' asked the solicitor.

'If you like to come outside we can have a go,' replied John Mitchell.

'Can you throw a stone from Melbost road end to Aignish corner?' was the response.

Murdo Campbell (Steel) from Bragar was the driver of this Bedford OB with a Mitchell-built body.
It can be seen that it has suffered from the poor post-war roads.

John Mitchell said he did not suggest that, but Aignish was the unpopular end of the beach.

John Mitchell was the winner on this occasion, the application by Hebridean Transport Ltd being refused.

The meeting, however, was not yet finished. Next, Hebridean Transport Ltd applied for a licence to operate summer tours to various parts of the island, to enable people to see the places of interest. It was claimed that people had come to Hebridean Transport after having been to John Mitchell and been unable to get tours from him. Another interesting debate ensued. John stated that he had held a licence for tours since 1932. He had a selection of 23 tours but he did not run them all together, as some were seldom asked for. He had no difficulty in fulfilling the demand, advertising his tours by bills and posters. He did not have to refuse people for want of space on his buses.

When it was then suggested that some competition for tours would do no harm, John Mitchell replied, 'There's no excitement about tours in Lewis, and the number of visitors is very small.' He conveyed the point that there was insufficient interest in tours for two companies to operate and that he did not want any competition, going as far as to say, 'I will do my best to keep them (Hebridean Transport Ltd) out.' John Mitchell's arguments again won the day and he was left to run his tours unopposed.

More new routes

John Mitchell also continued to expand his own services. A new route, started in July 1948, ran from Stornoway to Plasterfield. This was replaced less than two years later, in February 1950, by additional services, to Melbost, Plasterfield, Marybank and Newmarket, the Traffic Commissioners noting that John was always keen to accommodate residents in new housing schemes. He also applied to extend his Laxdale corner run to Tong corner, operating on a roughly two-hourly basis. A Tong resident supported this, saying that nearly everyone in the area was employed in Stornoway and with the proposed service they could get home for a quick lunch. John also intended to provide a church service bus.

When the Traffic Commissioners held their annual meeting on Lewis a year later in May 1948, once again they were not spared from John Mitchell's attention. A new company, Galson Stornoway Motor Services Ltd, was to be formed if their application for licences to run services proved successful. They wished to operate services between Barvas, Galson and Stornoway, to which John objected on the grounds that it would affect his services in the area. The applicants said they had tried not to encroach on John's Ness timetable by spreading their runs throughout the day, and that there was a demand for an increase in services. John responded by saying that if there had been demand for more services he would have heard about it, but he had received no representations. He also objected that some of the proposed timings would clash with his services, saying, 'The fact is, it's not their own runs they're interested in, but mine. It's the passengers they see in my buses they're after.'

There were also conflicting applications between the two companies for the West Side circular tour, for which John Mitchell had previously been granted a licence. In this case John intimated that he was not objecting to the runs where they did not affect his services. While his service went off the main road to allow tourists to see the Stones at Callanish, the new company would not do this, stating that 'residents in the rural areas wanted to get to Stornoway as quickly as possible, not to spend half an hour sitting looking at Callanish Stones.' Galson Motor Services Ltd also suggested a demand from people wanting to visit Stornoway for evening entertainment. It was then suggested by the Traffic Commissioners that as there was so large a measure of agreement between the two companies that they should get together and suitably adjust their timetables. When the meeting resumed the following day it was intimated that agreement had been reached between John Mitchell and Galson Motor Services Ltd on both the Ness and West Side services.

John Mitchell's next concern involved competing applications between himself and Hebridean Transport Ltd for a service to the new housing area at Plasterfield. John already had a service in the area and considered his new application, technically for a new service, to be merely an extension of the existing route, 'to link up the two arms of the town service.' Instead of an hourly service the people of Goathill and Sandwick would be provided with a bus approximately every thirty minutes. John Mitchell admitted that he had been approached by residents of Plasterfield, but that he had told them the road would have to be improved before he would provide a service. He added that he had advised the residents to contact the County Council regarding the road condition.

Following this the Plasterfield residents asked Hebridean Transport Ltd to provide a service; they immediately agreed to do so.

John Mitchell's Plasterfield service was further criticised because of its unpunctuality and because passengers did not always get a seat. To this rather feeble last complaint Mr Robertson, the Traffic

Two young ladies wait beside another bus owned by Western Lewis Coaches. JS 8350, an Austin
dating from 1949, clearly shows the owner's details on the back. This company ran in opposition
to John Mitchell until he bought the company in 1960.

Commissioner, remarked that standing was done on the mainland, in Aberdeen, in Glasgow and in London, and the people of Stornoway must get used to it too.

John Mitchell's last action in the 1940s was to take over the business of Donald Finlayson, one of the earliest operators of buses on the island. He had operated a competing service to Ness. He sold his business to John in December 1949, with the licences being transferred a month later. Gradually John Mitchell had eliminated much of his opposition and competition.

The 'stolen bus'

In October 1948, John Mitchell appeared in court in Stornoway. On this occasion, rather than being the accused, he was there to present evidence. It was another convoluted case, involving a former director of Lochs Motor Transport Ltd, Alexander D Maclean, who was charged with taking and driving away a motor vehicle without the owner's permission. The bus in question was one which John had ordered for Lochs Motor Transport Ltd. John Mitchell said in evidence that on 19 April, as he was preparing to leave for the mainland by plane, he was met by Mr Maclean at his house; the latter asked about the bus, which had arrived on the mail-boat the previous evening. John informed Maclean that he could not have the bus until it was paid for, but on returning to Lewis he discovered that the bus had been taken, without having been paid for.

On 27 April, John Mitchell saw the bus, carrying passengers to a football match at Goathill. He advised the driver that he was taking the bus back as it had not been paid for. The solicitor appearing on behalf of Maclean asked John if he agreed that a letter stating 'Your bus arrived by the mail-boat tonight, and I shall be glad if you will take delivery immediately,' had been sent from his office. John agreed. 'Who was the owner on 19th April?' asked the solicitor. 'I was,' replied John. The bus had been ordered on behalf of Lochs Motor Transport, he said, but it was not their property until it was paid for.

An employee of John Mitchell told how Maclean had come for the bus, and how John had phoned down earlier in the day saying Maclean was collecting it and to have the account ready. She gave Maclean the account and he said something to the effect that it would be paid on Friday. Maclean's solicitor said there was no corroboration of Mr Mitchell's statement, and, in any case, he did not see how John Mitchell could say that the bus had been taken without permission when he agreed that the words 'your bus' had been used in a letter to Lochs Motor Transport.

The Sheriff accepted John Mitchell's statement, but as it had not been corroborated, had to give his verdict as 'not proven.' The bus was returned to John Mitchell.

Problems with the weather

Problems operating buses due to severe weather conditions have already been mentioned, and in the years following the end of the Second World War there were also a number of occasions when services were interrupted.

The beginning of 1948 saw a severe spell of winter weather. The 'freeze-up' began on Sunday 4 January and lasted the whole of the following week. It was thought that in some parts of the island the roads were the worst for many years. One particularly bad stretch was south of Keose. John Mitchell's South Lochs bus did not manage to get through on the night of Friday the ninth, while the following day his Harris bus managed to get through and return again on Saturday morning. However it was unable to return to Harris that night, and on making a second attempt on the Sunday morning had to turn back as a section of the road had given way at Aline. John hired a Harris bus to meet the outgoing vehicle, and passengers and goods were transferred across the ravine from one bus to the other. This procedure was continued until the road was suitably restored with a temporary bridge.

A bus to Ness struggled to reach its destination, leaving Stornoway at 4pm and not reaching its destination until 10pm. The following day the 9am bus from Ness had to be abandoned at Barvas.

It was not often that weather affected bus services during the summer, but one occasion was in May 1954. Normally a number of Mitchell's Buses would be hired out for excursions on the May Holiday, but that day gale force winds swept the island during the morning, followed by torrential rain. Only two buses were hired, and there was no demand for the ordinary services.

Winter weather returned in January 1955 to cause problems when the island was hit by the worst snow storm experienced for many years. All the services became completely disorganised, with even the town services having to be cancelled. John Mitchell reported, 'So far none of my buses have reached town. The Balallan bus started off and got as far as Soval. I understand it has turned back. The town services are also held up. All the buses are stuck near their starting points.'

He continued, 'I don't think we have had such a complete hold up of the bus services since the Road Traffic Act came into force [in 1930]. There have been occasions when most of the services have been off,

A BIZARRE COURT CASE

In November 1949 John Mitchell was faced with a court case which was both bizarre and trivial. The report in the Stornoway Gazette was headed 'The Passengers Waited,' followed by a sub-heading, 'But Legally the Bus Wasn't Late.' What occurred in the court was reported as follows:

When John Mitchell, Motor Hirer, Stornoway, was charged in the Sheriff Court on Friday with failing to make a scheduled run on his Plasterfield service, two police constables, three passengers, and the conductress, all told the Court that the bus was thirty-five minutes late.

Mr J T Simpson, solicitor, for Mr Mitchell, asked no questions and called no witnesses. It was put to the two constables, 'Do you know that Mr Mitchell has a licence?'

'But that is not enough according to Lord Mackay,' said Mr Simpson, calling attention to a High Court judgement, which, he said, laid down the principle that the licence must be produced in Court.

'It is surely not to be presumed that Mr Mitchell is running a service without the authority of the Northern Scottish Area Traffic Commissioners,' commented the Fiscal.

'All we have in this case is a number of passengers who state that there was a bus at that time, and two policemen who say that they knew there was a bus at that time,' said Sheriff Miller.

'There was no production of the licence, so that it could be seen here. The fact that there was a legal requirement on the accused to run a service at 4 o'clock has not been proved in the best way, because there is no documentary evidence.'

The verdict was – not guilty.

Overleaf: The opposition – one of Western Lewis Coaches' buses waits for passengers in Cromwell Street, Stornoway.

but there has generally been one or two of the buses able to run, especially near the town.'

Later that week a bus meeting the mail boat at Stornoway left for Carloway shortly before 11pm – over three hours late. By four o'clock the following morning, with the passengers alternately pushing and digging, the bus had only got as far as Achmore, where it stuck completely. Passengers had to arouse the people of Achmore and Lochganvich by knocking on their doors to 'lodge' with them for the weekend. A few impatient passengers set off walking to Carloway, and were fortunately met by a lorry which had left that village to meet them. Three of the passengers, who worked in Stornoway and had been going home for the weekend, had a chilly and strenuous Sunday – they had to walk back to Stornoway from Achmore for work on Monday morning.

In 1958 snow struck again. On a Sunday in March a bus from Stornoway taking worshippers to the communion service in Barvas became stuck in deep drifts about two miles beyond the water works on the Barvas Moor. The driver had a spade and he dug the vehicle free, but found that he was going 'out of one drift into another.' One of the passengers walked back to the water works (just beyond Newmarket) and telephoned John Mitchell, who sent out a lorry which, after becoming stuck itself three times, managed to pull the bus clear. Both vehicles then returned to Stornoway, the passengers making no further attempt to reach their destination.

More dealings with the Traffic Commisssioners

The 1949 meeting of the Traffic Commissioners and the local bus operators opened, for once, with a topic other than licence applications: the state of the roads. The representatives of the Commissioners, Mr Robertson and Major Mitchell (no relation), had inspected the roads on the island and the former suggested that all operators should extend their running times by ten or fifteen minutes to take account of the state of the roads. This would enable the drivers to drive with a degree of caution and save the wear and tear of the buses. John Mitchell thought the only real solution was that the roads be improved, otherwise there would soon be no buses available for anyone. Mr Robertson agreed, stating that he had already made representations to the County Council about the Tolsta Road.

The deteriorating state of the Lewis roads arose again when the Traffic Commissioners convened for their meeting in May 1950. The road transport services on the island were said to be facing a crisis. The Commissioners had found a further deterioration in the state of the roads and it was thought that, far from applying for additional services, the operators might have to curtail or even withdraw completely services on some of the side roads.

'Frankly we are surprised that the operators are able to maintain services on some of the roads they are in such bad condition,' declared Mr Robertson, the Traffic Commissioner. 'We are not responsible for the state of the roads,' he continued. 'That is the concern of the County Council and the Ministry of Transport. We shall, however, report to the proper quarter of the conditions under which transport is carried on in Lewis. The wear and tear on buses in Lewis is excessive and much beyond that on the mainland.'

He went on to mention that wages had risen, tyres and spare parts had increased in price, and in addition there was the recent increase in the price of petrol. He considered some revision of fares to be necessary if the bus services were to be kept running. He understood that the bus operators had met and agreed on fare increases, adding, 'All that I can say is that if fares are raised much higher there will be a danger of a serious drop in passengers and the extra revenue will not be forthcoming.'

John Mitchell then said that the rise in the cost of tyres and spare parts was not what the operators were really up against. It was the conditions under which they were operating. 'It is a shocking state of affairs when you are called on by the Ministry of Transport to keep your vehicles in a condition which it is quite impossible to do. I do not think it is possible for any operator to continue under the present conditions whether fares are raised or not. The time is not far off when we will not be able to keep our buses on the roads. The roads are beyond anything that anybody could dream of.'

This situation was underlined when John Mitchell came to apply for renewal of his licence for the West Side circular service. Mr Robertson, the Traffic Commissioner, pointed out that the service had not operated since the previous January. This was because part of the road was under repair and in a very bad state, making it impossible to operate buses on it. It was not known when the service could be resumed, but John wished to renew the licence in the hope the service could be started again. Mr Robertson asked if there was any possibility of the road, between seven and eight miles in length, being repaired before the next sitting of the Commissioners; the reply was that at the present rate of progress the answer was no. 'But if they concentrated on it, it could be finished in a week,' replied Major Mitchell, acting for John.

Overleaf: Schoolchildren are picked up on Matheson Road,
at the junction with Springfield Road.

In 1951 John Mitchell re-applied to the Traffic Commissioners for the licence to operate his West Side circular service. It must be assumed that by now the road condition must have been satisfactorily improved. John intended to run the services during the summer, operating three buses a day from Stornoway via Achmore and three via Barvas on alternative days. He said, 'I am not at all looking forward to any gain by resuming these services. It serves only a small few who come home in the summer months and want to visit relatives in the west side villages.' Asked why he intended not to operate during the winter he replied, 'Because I know it will be uneconomic.'

'You will agree that you will take traffic from the objectors (Western Lewis Coaches) on the Shawbost-Stornoway and Carloway-Stornoway routes?'

'Yes.'

The objectors claimed that John Mitchell's service was not now being run for tourists but was running from village to village, and that their company, amalgamated from several West Side operators, had shown a profit for the first time and that any competition would be detrimental to them. 'If Mr Mitchell gets this run he knows as well as I do that this company is finished,' declared the manager of Western Lewis Coaches.

Trouble with the Point Communion buses

On the island of Lewis the Presbyterian churches hold Communion Services twice a year. The services are attended by people from all over the island. During the 1950s as many as 2,000 would attend the services in Point, and special buses were laid on to take people to the services. These were provided by different bus companies, including that of John Mitchell, who would use up to five of his buses. Normally these buses operated without problems but on several occasions disputes arose between John Mitchell and another bus company, Hebridean Transport Ltd, over the provision of these extra bus services.

In 1950 some of the disputes had to be settled at Stornoway Sheriff Court. On the first occasion, John Mitchell was accused of operating more coaches than his licence permitted. Following discussion regarding the technicalities of John's licence, the Sheriff then gave his judgement; John Mitchell was admonished, the Sheriff adding that there was little in the case and that it was just the competitors keeping an eye on each other.

Four months later John Mitchell and the managing director of Hebridean Transport Ltd were in court again. During the hearing

John was asked about his motives in bringing about the complaints, it being thought that as he had recently been convicted for contravening his own tours licence, he might be looking for revenge. The court then heard that John had watched to check that a particular service had operated on time. After hearing the evidence, based on the time that the bus would have taken from Stornoway to Point, the Sheriff, calculated that the bus must have made a pretty quick journey. He pointed out, 'It must have left on time, and that is a remarkable thing in Stornoway. The only thing that starts on time in Stornoway is the Church – and that starts like the crack of doom!' He then said that he did not care what John Mitchell's motive was in watching the Hebridean buses and that he was as entitled to do that as anyone else. After weighing up the evidence he found that the bus in question did not leave at all, found the charge proven, and fined Macmillan £3.

A second charge was as convoluted as the first. This time the charge was that Hebridean Transport Ltd ran an unauthorised bus service, from Bayble to Stornoway, picking up from a Communion service, passengers who, according to John Mitchell, should have been on his bus. John Mitchell had again been watching the departure times of the opposition, and his evidence was accepted resulting in the charge being proven and Hebridean Transport Ltd being fined £5. The Sheriff added, 'I hope that this is not the general habit in running transport here. It seems to be in a chaotic condition.'

It was not long before John Mitchell and Hebridean Transport Ltd were sparring again about buses at Communion time. This time they met in Inverness at a sitting of the Transport Commissioners, only months after the previous cases. Hebridean Transport Ltd had lodged an application to vary their services from Stornoway to Garrabost. The objection raised by Mitchell was on the grounds that the application

Running repairs are carried out on the Ness bus outside the garage.

In 1951 John was involved in a court case with a passenger who had been injured when her coat had become caught in the door of a bus. This is a view of a more modern bus, but it shows a folding door similar to the one responsible for the accident.

was 'vague and lacking in specification.' Mr Robertson, the Traffic Commissioner, wished to hear the case as he was anxious to have the matter settled 'once and for all.'

Hebridean Transport Ltd argued that the reason for the application was that at Communion times the company carried people to the church services on their regular runs, but as the services ended at different times they wished to take the passengers back shortly after the services ended, thus saving the church-goers, many of whom were elderly, from having to wait unduly in varying weather conditions. This was the reason for the variation in the timetables.

The argument had stemmed from a previous occasion when Hebridean Transport Ltd alleged that after the end of a church service, John Mitchell had insisted on picking up passengers who had arrived on buses of Hebridean Transport Ltd. He was not entitled to do so with a tour and excursion licence. The representative of Hebridean Transport Ltd pointed out that John Mitchell 'seemed to think he was the only operator out of Stornoway but where he had got that impression no one knew. He had not the sole right to services out of Stornoway although he was the only touring operator there.' Clearly there was little love lost between the two companies, and John was certainly unwilling to concede anything to his opposition.

The Traffic Commissioners' main aim was to ensure that the travelling public was suitably catered for. It was initially stated that they wanted to sort the matter out there and then. It was perhaps not surprising that after the tangle of evidence presented, the Commissioners decided that, as there was no great urgency in the matter as the next

This cartoon appeared in the Stornoway Gazette when John increased fares in 1953. Clearly this was not a popular move.

Recognisable by its white colour, JS 8232 was the 'stolen' bus.

Communion season in Point was not until the following spring, no immediate decision was to be made. Instead, they decided to reserve judgement until they next visited Stornoway, when they would have an opportunity of hearing at first hand the views of ministers and other interested parties.

There is not any evidence regarding the conclusion of these cases, but as no further reports appeared, it must be assumed that eventually differences were settled and peace returned to the two bus companies and their services for the Church Communion worshippers.

Failing to attend to her passengers – a court case

An accident involving one of Mitchell's buses in February 1951 led to yet another court hearing the following June. On this occasion a passenger alighting from a bus in Bayhead had caught her coat in the door of the bus and then been dragged fifty yards along the road when the bus started. The conductress of the bus was accused of failing to attend to the safety of her passengers.

The passenger told the Court that when she left the bus the conductress was sitting in a back seat talking to a passenger. The conductress claimed she was collecting fares at the back of the bus, but this was not accepted by the Sheriff, who said, 'The conductress acted in a selfish and indifferent way.' There was no signalling system on the bus, the bell having been out of order.

The passenger described the accident. 'I alighted from the bus and the next thing I knew I was being dragged along.' The door, at the front of the bus, was hinged in the middle and folded inwards. The passenger said it was very stiff and she had a struggle before it opened. 'Where was the conductress?' asked the Fiscal. 'At the other end of the bus speaking to a young boy,' was the reply.

The passenger had then been dragged on her right elbow, which was grazed to the bone, and her clothes were torn. She was asked, 'You are quite sure you did not close the door as you got off?'

'I did not.'

'I put it to you that you gave the driver an indication that you were off the bus and that you touched the door to close it as it started off.'

'I have no recollection of doing that,' the passenger replied. Another passenger said that he had heard no signal for the driver to start. The driver, however, informed the Court that someone inside the bus had given him a signal. He claimed the passenger had closed the door herself when she jumped off. He had stopped the bus when he heard a woman screaming in the back.

The conductress then gave evidence. She maintained that she was collecting fares at the back of the bus when the passenger alighted. 'Before I got to the door she had already alighted.'

On being asked if she had gone to the door to see if she was clear of the bus, the conductress replied, 'I never thought of that.'

The defending solicitor submitted that although the conductress was required to look after her passengers she also had to collect fares. 'If a passenger takes it into her head to open the door and alight, she does it at her own risk. If she wants to stick by the letter of the law she must stand there until the door is opened for her.'

The Sheriff accepted that it was feasible that the passenger had closed the door herself, but 'the point is this conductress was not paying any attention to her duties . . . she was sitting at the back of the bus, not collecting fares.' The conductress was found guilty of failing to attend to the safety of her passengers and fined £4.

The Traffic Commissioners again

Having on many occasions had to fight against the traffic Commissioners, it must have come as a welcome change to have them on his side, as happened in 1953. Running costs continued to increase and it was becoming apparent that running bus services on the island at a profit was becoming steadily more difficult. Fare increases of roughly two pence in the shilling had already been introduced, although increased fares did not necessarily mean increased revenue, as the number of cars was gradually increasing. The Chairman of the

1953 Traffic Commissioners' meeting in Stornoway was sympathetic to the situation and warned that services might deteriorate and return to the conditions which existed twenty years earlier. John Mitchell was one of five operators who were asking for fare increases. In a number of cases the County Council was objecting on the grounds that the increases were excessive.

A Councillor from Ness objected strongly to the increased fares on John Mitchell's Stornoway-Ness route. The fares were already too high and the general state of the service did not justify a further increase. She based her list of complaints on the state of the buses. They were old and dilapidated, on several occasions she had rain splashing on her, and on one bus an iron wedge was required to keep the door shut. Further the vehicles were overcrowded 'to such an extent that it would not be allowed anywhere but on the island of Lewis, and even if one was lucky enough to get a seat it was a wooden slatted one that was not at all comfortable.'

In answer to these complaints John Mitchell said that the fault really lay with the roads. 'There had not been a bus or a door invented which would stand up to the running on Lewis roads.' Admitting that faults did arise, he said the buses were examined and maintained regularly and defects rectified then. The problem of overcrowding was dealt with putting on a duplicate bus. The wooden seats were justified by the facts that they stood up better to wear and tear and were more easily repaired and were, in fact, the only seats suitable for the conditions. 'If I had my way,' said John, 'I would have wooden seats on all the buses.'

A comment was then passed that such seats were 'behind the times,' to which John Mitchell countered, 'The conditions we are working under are very much behind the times.' A decision was deferred on John's application, but the Traffic Commissioner indicated that fare increases would be granted, but perhaps not the full amount applied for.

Judging by the lack of controversy at later Traffic Commissioners' meetings, the rest of the decade can be considered as a time of stability. John Mitchell's buses now served much of Lewis. As well as operating the town services, his buses reached Tolsta, Ness, the West Side and Lochs. South Lochs, Uig and Bernera were the only districts that he did not run to. In addition he had services reaching to the southern tip of Harris.

Overleaf: This Bedford OWB with Duple body was owned by Back-Stornoway Transport Ltd between 1948 and 1951, when it passed into the ownership of John Mitchell, who had bought out the company. It is pictured here on North Beach Street, opposite the Lewis Hotel. The photo was taken before 1957, which was when the wooden building behind the bus, the MNI office, was demolished.

11. PROBLEMS WITH THE TOLSTA SERVICE

During early post-war years the services to Back and Tolsta were never far from the minds of John Mitchell, the Traffic Commissioners and the inhabitants of the townships along the route. In 1947, the services were operated, in competition, by John and a newly formed local company, Back-Stornoway Transport Ltd. This company was the result of mergers of the three companies which had been competing on the Stornoway-Back service. Back Motor Transport (operated by John Maciver since 1931), John & Angus Murray (the former having started as early as 1925 and with a stage carriage licence from 1931) and George Stewart (first service in 1924, first licence in 1931) set up a co-operative venture in July 1947. Their idea was to remove any competition on the one route, although they did have John Mitchell to contend with.

John Mitchell had submitted an objection to the Back company's application to add some new services, the latter justifying them as allowing afternoon shopping in Stornoway, enabling people to get back to town after an evening round of golf at Coll, letting those who finished work at 5pm get home (most did not finish until 6pm), and enabling people from the country to attend the second house at the Playhouse Cinema in Stornoway. All these seemed more than reasonable to the Commissioners, and they were generally in favour of this application, but were aware that John Mitchell also served this area and he should not be disadvantaged. Various changes were made in the timetable, but most of the alterations asked for were refused. John Mitchell was going to do his best to make sure that none of his services had to suffer from any competition, suggesting that, as he had earlier claimed, that he did consider that he had, or should have, a monopoly.

It would appear that there was insufficient traffic to support the two companies and that common sense had prevailed, for in 1948 John Mitchell and Back-Stornoway Transport Ltd commenced sharing the service to Tolsta. The shared service did not always run smoothly, resulting in the two operators appearing at the Sherriff Court in Stornoway in March 1948. A dispute had arisen over the Back bus service: Back-Stornoway Transport was charged with running a contract bus at or about the same time as a regular service operated by John Mitchell.

It was stated in the court that because of dissatisfaction with the service provided by John Mitchell, mill workers from the Back district decided to place a contract for a nightly service to Back at 6pm, taking the passengers close to their homes instead of dropping them off at road ends, leaving them with a walk of anything up to a mile. A total of twenty-three people were travelling by that bus. On occasions, when these passengers used Mitchell's bus, the conductress asked them to stand to make room for the Tolsta passengers. John Mitchell said that there were now three buses going in the same direction at 6.10pm, and he had licences which varied so that his services could go off the main road, providing the same service as the Back-Stornoway bus. The latter's bus left Stornoway a few minutes before Mitchell's, who complained to the Traffic Commissioners about it because he was losing passengers.

The charge was found proved, the Sheriff saying that the run was taking place too frequently to be considered a special hire. Once a month would have been acceptable, but the fact it ran daily and every evening just prior to Mitchell's service, meant he had to find it a breach of the Road Traffic Act. The accused was, however, admonished.

The amount of traffic on the Tolsta route was insufficient for the two operators to continue, and in June 1951 John Mitchell purchased Back-Stornoway Transport Ltd, giving him a monopoly of the services on that route.

The 'deplorable state' of the Tolsta road was the cause of damage to John Mitchell's buses, and led to another appearance of John in court. When asked at a Traffic Commissioners' meeting if he knew of any other operator in the United Kingdom who spent the same amount as he did on the upkeep of vehicle springs, he replied, 'I don't think they exist.'

Then in June 1948, the damage done to John Mitchell's buses by the poor condition of the Tolsta road led to a court case. John Mitchell was fined £10 for having in commission a bus which had no horn, no efficient hand-brake, no windscreen wiper, and no road fund licence shown.

The Fiscal stated that the police had received complaints from passengers about the state of the buses, and shortly after a constable examined a bus while it was standing on Cromwell Street Quay before setting off for North Tolsta. He found it short of the items with which John Mitchell was charged.

The court was told that the bus was a substitute put on in an emergency, because if John Mitchell had not put on some bus he would then have been charged for failing to make a scheduled run. The state of the buses was caused by the condition of the North Tolsta road. He continued, 'So much so that when the Traffic Commissioners were here they inspected the road, and they have now intimated to the Road Department of the Road Authority that unless something is done to improve the condition of the road the road licence will be withdrawn altogether and the service lost.'

John Mitchell was described as being between the devil and the deep sea. He could not obtain spare parts for his buses, nor could he get new buses.

When the Sheriff commented that it was a serious thing not to have a horn to warn others, Mr Mitchell's solicitor replied, 'These buses are so badly knocked about by the road that you can hear them three miles away.'

'It's a silencer they need,' remarked the Fiscal.

'I don't think you could hear the sound of the horn above the noises the bus was making,' added the solicitor.

In 1952 John Mitchell antagonized the people of North Tolsta by proposing to reduce the number of services to the village. Objections were based on the fact that Point, with a similar population had twelve runs a day, more than twice the number to Tolsta. In addition the run that John proposed to drop, at 4.30pm, was thought to be the only run that did pay, while the late bus had also been seen with so many passengers on it that two intending lady passengers had decided to spend the night in town. When asked about the capacity of the bus a local Councillor replied, 'I've been on it with 52 in it – and a policeman!'

As well as the reduction in services they were concerned about the fact that no tickets were issued on the service. This meant that passengers making a double trip had to pay the half-crown single fare each time, instead of the normal return fare of 4s 3d. An 'ultimatum' stating that no fares would be paid on the bus unless tickets were issued was wired to the Traffic Commissioners; it read, 'Mitchell's service to North Tolsta issues no tickets. Prosecute or rectify. After seven days – no tickets no fares.' Within twenty-four hours the following reply was received: 'Mitchell's office has given assurance tickets now obtained and being issued for single and return fares. Representations on time-tables now under consideration.'

The Tolsta service was to be further cut back by ceasing to operate buses into the village of Tong, about half-way between Stornoway and Tolsta, which was then a cul-de-sac road. This proved very unpopular

A Bedford SB negotiating the bridge at Glen Tolsta.

with the villagers, who in September 1952 called a meeting to protest against the cuts. John Mitchell explained that it was not economic to route his buses into Tong, remaining adamant about this despite many questions being put to him. He suggested that if the road through Tong was continued for a few hundred yards to re-join the main road he would run his buses through the village. Villagers thought that it would take 'years to get the various authorities to approve and carry out the plan, although it would involve only some few hundred yards of road.' At a meeting held by the inhabitants of Tong its chairman stated, 'Mr Mitchell presented his case to the meeting very well and kept to his point. But he made no concessions. It was either "take it or leave it".' He went on to say, 'Our very existence as a community is threatened if we cannot get a bus service resumed.'

Today some of the Tolsta buses, no longer operated by John Mitchell, are routed through Tong, using the short stretch of road that was built to provide a through route; it took many years to reach a settlement agreeable to all.

Overleaf: Passengers board a bus for Tolsta in the 1950s. The bus is a Bedford with a Duple body. It appears to have suffered some damage to its body, perhaps due to the condition of the road to Tolsta at that time.

12. THE CHURCH STREET PROBLEM

Church Street in Stornoway is a busy street running at right angles to Cromwell Street. Where it joins Cromwell Street it is on a steep hill, and the roadway is narrow, only wide enough for two cars to pass with great care. On either side of the roadway there is a very narrow pavement, hardly wide enough for two people to walk abreast, and buildings rise up immediately beyond the pavement. Further up the street where it becomes slightly wider, it is crossed at right angles by Kenneth Street and Keith Street. All of these streets have always carried a considerable amount of traffic.

Church Street proved a thorn in the side of John Mitchell for thirteen years.

Buses stopping outside a house – a mountain out of a molehill

The first problem arose in July 1942. Mrs Murdo Matheson, a resident of Church Street, complained to the Town Council about the inconvenience of buses stopping outside her house to set down and pick up passengers. As can be seen from what followed, a molehill developed into a mountain. The matter was called to the notice of the Council Highways Committee and was taken up by ex-Provost Smith who stated that buses in Stornoway for a long time had been running without regular stopping places and he considered that it might be desirable if regular stopping places were made to suit the convenience of the public. He continued, 'A party [Mrs Matheson] came to me today and told me that they tried for some considerable time to get some amelioration of the conditions under which they exist themselves. They said they spoke some time ago to two of the magistrates in the absence of the Provost, and they wrote the Council and the Council threw the onus on the police and the police threw it on someone else. That is not right; that is not the way to deal with the ratepayers,' added the ex-Provost. 'This Council should have given an undertaking to have the matter dealt with by getting in touch with the Traffic Commissioners, pointing out that there are suitable stopping places in the near neighbourhood, where buses could stop without inconvenience to anyone.'

There are no photographs of buses negotiating Church Street, but this view of Francis Street at the Post Office shows the difficulties of operating buses on the narrow streets of Stornoway.

'It seems to me that this matter has not been given even that modest consideration which it deserves, and it is up to the Council to do something,' he continued. He proposed that they ask the owner of the buses concerned to do something about it, and, failing that, approach the Traffic Commissioners.

The matter was then taken up by Baillie Mrs Fraser, who said that after Mrs Matheson spoke to her she phoned John Mitchell and pointed out to him the unfairness of having these buses stopping outside her house filling it with fumes, and John promised that he would speak to his drivers.

Ex-Baillie Tolmie then suggested that the best solution was to put up notices 'the same as for parking places.'

'You cannot do that,' said the Town Clerk.

'I can't understand that,' said ex-Baillie Tolmie. 'The Town Clerk says we can't do that. We are the Local Authority here and we can do these things. We can make the bus-drivers stop in certain places, just the same as make them go certain places. How is it that in Glasgow one sees bus stops here and there, and you have to run to them like the very dickens to catch your bus? If they have the authority in cities to do that, surely we have it in the burgh.'

Baillie Maclean, while having sympathy for the residents, said that the council had to remember that the buses were carrying out a very necessary service, and the Council should do their best also to help the bus owner and the drivers.

The Town Clerk explained that neither the Town Council nor the police had any authority to set up stopping places. This had to be done by the Traffic Commissioners, and the only action the Council could take was to make representations to that body.

It was unanimously agreed, however, that John Mitchell be approached, and that failing a satisfactory arrangement with him, the matter should be taken to the Traffic Commissioners. The final outcome of the 'problem' is not known, but it shows how what starts as a minor complaint can become blown out of proportion, as happened on a number of occasions involving John Mitchell's buses.

Downpipes carried away by bus

The problem of buses using Church Street re-appeared in the autumn of 1948. In September a statement was made at the Town Council Finance Committee meeting, stating that downpipes had been swept off houses on Church Street caused by buses mounting the pavement due to the narrowness of the street. As a result, it was recommended that the Police be asked for a report on the situation at the foot of Church Street, with suggestions for alleviating it. It was pointed out that the situation had been getting worse as the bus traffic had increased since the building of new houses at Plasterfield. One suggestion put forward was to have smaller buses on the Goathill service, which operated up and down Church Street, which would feed larger ones on the Laxdale-Sandwick service. A suggestion was also put forward that the lower part of the street might be closed to heavy traffic.

The Police report was presented to the Town Council in October 1948 by Superintendent Maciver. It stated, 'The public service vehicle route now followed throughout town by Mr John Mitchell is, I think, the best that could be followed if the needs of the inhabitants of the town, its suburbs and satellite villages are to be taken into account. All the main centres of population are catered for, as are the shopping centres.' The report pointed out that if the service was re-routed by any of the possible alternatives, then either its usefulness to the public would be nil, or there would be danger spots just as great as the one at the foot of Church Street.

The report continued, 'The present route via Church Street is the natural one – Church Street junctions with Kenneth Street, Keith Street, Lewis Street and Matheson Road are approximately equidistant from the north and south ends of these streets. It was impracticable to make Church Street between Cromwell Street and Kenneth Street a one way street because heavy vehicles passing stationary vehicles discharging or uplifting goods would still have to mount the pavement irrespective of which way the traffic was permitted to flow. Stationary heavy goods vehicles were the main cause of the trouble on Church Street, and not the service buses.'

Regarding the suggestion that smaller buses might be used on the town service by John Mitchell, Superintendent Maciver did not think that would solve the problem either. He thought that most if not all of the small buses in use on Lewis were of equal width as the large ones.

The question of routing buses through Kenneth Street was also dismissed, Superintendent Maciver suggesting that a large number of passengers deposited near the Kenneth Street-Church Street corner and walking down Church Street would be exposed to more danger than if carried in a bus. Furthermore he considered that on one hand 'if this part of Church Street were to be reserved for one class of traffic, say, Public Service vehicles, a hardship would be imposed on traders who have business premises there, but, on the other hand, if it were to be reserved for goods vehicles only, a hardship would be imposed on those members of the public who presently use the town bus service.'

Finally the report suggested that if John Mitchell's town service was to continue to follow the present route the stopping places at the foot of Church Street should be at least twenty yards further away from the junction. From this it can be seen that the existing service up and down Church Street was to continue.

Church Street a safe place?

The saga of Church Street was not, however, at an end. In March 1951, The Highways Committee of Stornoway Town Council invited Police Superintendent Maciver and John Mitchell to a meeting to continue discussion of the Church Street problem. The meeting was to last almost two hours.

While the findings of Superintendent Maciver's previous report had suggested retaining the Church Street service, this had not been seen as satisfactory by some councillors, concerned with safety aspects. The Superintendent had to defend his view, stating that he had 'never said Church Street was a safe place,' nor had he said that it was not dangerous. He stated that he had taken into account not only the question of safety but also the convenience of the public when saying that Church Street was the obvious street for the bus service. The report presented a factual account of the dilemma: that of safety for the public, or their convenience regarding people travelling.

At the meeting these two conflicting points were discussed. It was suggested that the Council acquire property at the corner of Kenneth Street and Scotland Street, allowing widening to take place, but John Mitchell thought that corner would still be dangerous. A new anti-clockwise circular service was proposed which would mean using Church Street in one direction only. John Mitchell's response to this suggestion was that by removing that part of the service one danger would be done away with, but others would be created. The amended service would not cater for the people between Nicolson Road and Goathill, missing out the whole of Goathill. From a traffic point of view there could be no objection to the route but John Mitchell added, 'It would be very unpopular from the public point of view.'

The suggestion was then mooted of turning the bus from Goathill on to Matheson Road, down Mackenzie Street and on to Bayhead. Mackenzie Street was considered to be a wide street with a gentle gradient, and buses could still deposit passengers at the foot of Church Street as before. John Mitchell though that if Church Street was to be barred to his buses this would be the safest alternative.

Another proposal was for a service from South Beach by James Street and Matheson Road to Goathill, returning by Matheson Road and Bayhead, not using Church Street at all. This was followed with the idea of a 'perimeter' route, going out by Macaulay Road and then by Sandwick Road, Mossend and Goathill before returning down Church Street. This final motion was the one which the meeting agreed upon, in spite of the fact that buses would still be using Church Street in one direction.

The corners in Church Street are dangerous

That the corners in Church Street were dangerous was demonstrated less than a month later when one of Mitchell's buses was involved in a collision with a car at the junction of Church Street and Lewis Street. It was another of those complex Stornoway cases, the Sheriff stating, 'This case is so confused that it is impossible to say that any theory is wrong.'

The charge in the case was for careless driving by the bus driver; the charge was eventually found not proven, which is not surprising when the details of the case are seen.

The car was going south along Lewis Street as the bus made its way up Church Street. The bus driver told the police his story. 'I was just coming up Church Street in third gear. I sounded my horn, looked left and the next thing I knew I was on top of the cove [Stornoway slang for a man]. I was not travelling fast, about fifteen miles an hour.'

A sketch made by the police showed the car close to the kerb on the south side of the east part of Church Street with the bus about a yard away and at approximately right angles to the car. The offside of the car had been pushed in and the bumper, headlamps and radiator of the bus damaged. The impression was that the bus had pushed the car about a yard up Church Street.

The driver of the car told the court that he was travelling about ten miles an hour as he approached the junction. The road was perfectly clear to the left and straight ahead. He looked down Church Street and saw nothing. 'Then I saw a bus coming and I had a second or a second and a half to throw myself from the driving seat into the passenger seat opposite before I was struck.'

'Did you apply your brakes?' asked the Fiscal.

'I don't think I had time to do anything but save my own body.' On being asked he said he had sounded his horn, and that he had not heard the engine or the horn of the bus.

The next witness was the conductress of the bus. The Sheriff, for some reason, described her as 'an ill-mannered cat,' and declared, 'It has been perfectly clear since you took the oath that you have come here with no intention of telling the truth, and then you shout at people in an insulting way.' She put the speed of the bus at twelve or thirteen miles an hour, and denied telling the police that it was more than that. She said the bus was well across the junction when she saw the car.

The accused was the sole defence witness. He told the Court that his windscreen was very wet and, apart from the part cleaned by the wiper, he could not see clearly. Questioned about the dullness of the windows, he declared, 'They're not safe, you might as well be driving a hearse.'

In his summing up, the streets and corners of Stornoway came in for some criticism. 'I am of the opinion that Stornoway has worse corners than any other place I have seen. In a place like this all the drivers should be tip-top but they are otherwise . . . One point in favour of this prosecution was that it had shown what could happen at a corner like this.' John Mitchell and the Superintendent Maciver could have warned him of this two years earlier!

As well as illustrating the difficulties incurred by John Mitchell's buses negotiating Church Street, the case illustrates well the complexities and difficulties of those days in carrying out justice in a town where everyone knows each other, where the truth is often a grey area and where the standard of vehicles on the road might well have been below that which was acceptable elsewhere.

Re-routing again

In November 1951 the Stornoway Gazette warned 'There will be opposition from Stornoway Town Council when Mr John Mitchell's licence for the town bus service comes up for renewal before the Traffic Commissioners next June.' Earlier in the year Mr Mitchell had refused to re-route his service, having been asked once more not to use Church Street. The Dean of Guild claimed that Mr Mitchell had made no effort to co-operate in finding a new route, in spite of his own admission that buses often had to mount the pavement to pass other vehicles on Church Street.

A variety of suggestions were made by members of the Council: oppose renewal of the licence, close Church Street to vehicles (although it was thought this might lead to the complete withdrawal of the service by John Mitchell), get someone else to run the service, or establish a municipal service. Finally it was decided that the first step should be to oppose renewal of Mr Mitchell's licence. 'I think we would have a fair measure of success because I don't see that any Traffic Commissioners could possibly condone this, especially when it is necessary for a bus on a steep incline to mount a footpath three feet wide,' said the Dean of Guild. 'There has been no accident so far, but that is entirely due to the agility of the pedestrians in getting out of the way into doorways and closes.'

The Town Council duly took their objection to the next meeting of the Traffic Commissioners, held in Stornoway in May 1952. Their case was not helped by the Police Superintendent stating that since the bus service began in 1932 there had been no accident in Church Street resulting in death or injury in which any of Mr Mitchell's buses had been involved. Then, after lengthy cross-examination, the Chairman, Mr Robertson, came up with a new solution. He was going to renew John Mitchell's licence for only one year instead of the normal three, stating that he had been for a walk round the new housing scheme at Leverhulme Drive and considering that it would be an advantage to re-route the service down this road when it was completed.

However, even after two years the problem had still not been solved. In May 1954 the Town Council again lodged an objection to the application to the Traffic Commissioners by John Mitchell to continue operating the Plasterfield-Laxdale service by way of Church Street. The Town Clerk asked John to make a real attempt to solve the issue. The latter stated that coming down Leverhulme Drive would add considerably to his expenses. He calculated the costs at a minimum of 1/6 a mile. 'That service is only washing its face as it is,' he remarked. Mr Robertson, for the Commissioners, said that with

Unlike most of the buses, which were Bedfords, this one was an Albion, AV 8329, built in 1936, although not purchased by John until 1947. It is seen here on a wet South Beach Street in Stornoway. A bus of this size would have had difficulty negotiating Church Street.
Overleaf: The same bus pictured in 1973. Like many island buses it ended its days being used as a shed, slowly sinking into the moor at Barvas.

the increase in occupied housing in the Plasterfield area, Mr Mitchell would, 'need to put on his thinking cap about the whole arrangement.' As had happened the previous year, John Mitchell was granted a renewal of his licence for one year without the Church Street problem being solved.

A year later and the matter was still on the agenda at the Traffic Commissioners' meeting in August 1955. The Town Council was still pushing for the route to be changed away from Church Street, with Leverhulme Drive again the preferred option, with even a trial period being suggested. John Mitchell was having nothing to do with it. He said he was not in a mood to make any alterations, because he did not see how it was going to benefit the community or himself. The chairman of the meeting said there was no doubt a bus service to run on a street such as Church Street on the mainland would not be granted a permit if there was an alternative route. He decided then to grant the trial period asked for by the Town council, fixing it for three months; the service would run up, but not down, Church Street.

The route was eventually changed with the journey from Cromwell Street being re-routed via Stag Road; the inward journey still used Church Street, but at least buses would no longer have to pass there. Eventually both journeys were directed away from Church Street. The Church Street problem had at long last been laid to rest.

13. POST-WAR EXPANSION OF THE GARAGE, BUT NOT WITHOUT MORE PROBLEMS

John Mitchell's business steadily grew during the late 1940s and the two following decades, as it had done during the 1930s and through the years of the Second World War.

In 1949, John Mitchell was able to develop his garage business by extending the buildings on his existing site, where an accident repair bodyshop was created. This time there were no issues with the Trust. He continued to retain and develop the Vauxhall-Bedford agency which he had started before the Second World War. Vauxhall cars and Bedford lorries supplied by John had become a common sight throughout the island. In 1950, John Mitchell also took on the Standard Triumph agency.

By the 1950s he was operating over twenty buses, this number exceeding thirty at the start of the next decade. He also operated a number of lorries, cars for hire and a twenty-four hour breakdown service with four recovery vehicles of different sizes, known locally as 'Daddy Bear', 'Mammy Bear', 'Baby Bear' and 'Snowy Bear.' All of these activities were known in Lewis as 'Mitchell's Garage.'

John also became involved in another enterprise in the 1950s when he bought the quarry and accompanying stone-crushing business at Carnish, in the Uig district on the west side of Lewis. As well as the quarrying and crushing of stone he had a fleet of lorries delivering material to all parts of the island. These developments were important to John, with his son-in-law Sandy reporting that, 'he operated a quarry in Uig for a few years and material was used in the construction of military sites, eg radar installations or an aerodrome. He would always take us to the quarry – his pride and joy that he had got it operational.' At that time, it seemed that it was the quarry which interested John more than his garage and bus operations.

Around 1954 John suffered a heart attack, was bed-ridden for about six months and made a decision to reduce his workload. With his son Ian having finished his motor training in Luton and now working in the garage, John also began to step back from the business in the 1950s – the plan was that Ian would eventually take over the garage.

Top: Two of the breakdown trucks and a Dormobile van in a posed photograph.
Bottom: The smaller tow truck. No opportunity was lost to advertise Mitchell's services and vehicle franchises.

FOR SALE
Cars, Vans, Utilecons,
Lorries and Buses.
New and Second hand.
John Mitchell
BEDFORD DEALER
STORNOWAY

Busy on business . . .
or idly inclined . . .
the car you'll enjoy
is a **Vauxhall**

Increasing Vauxhall production means favourable delivery.
May we demonstrate Vauxhall value on the road?

JOHN MITCHELL
VAUXHALL — BEDFORD DEALER
STORNOWAY
TELEPHONE : 94

YOU GET MORE DONE
YOU SEE MORE SIGHTS
WHEN YOU . . . .
RENT-A-CAR
CHAUFFEUR or
SELF DRIVE

We will meet your boat or plane, and will be
glad to supply maps, routes, and any other
information you may require.

ASK FOR FREE LEAFLET

MITCHELL'S TRANSPORT
AND
PARCEL SERVICE
BAYHEAD STREET · STORNOWAY
TEL 94

Mitchell's advertised a variety of the services in the Stornoway Gazette in the 1950s.
Overleaf: This 1960s view of the garage displays many of the services then provided
– BP petrol, Vauxhall, Bedford, Standard-Triumph and Volkswagen franchises,
MoT provision and AA and RAC patronage.

Further disputes

In March 1958, a possible dispute between John Mitchell and, this time, the Town Council, was averted when the latter decided against instigating alterations to the road pattern outside the garage. The scheme would have involved the acquisition of three plots of land by the Council, one of which belonged to John. He was prepared to offer the land free of charge, in the interest of the public, but he informed the Highways Committee of the Town Council that he was convinced that the scheme would 'not be an improvement but rather a source of danger and inconvenience to all road users.' In addition, it would deprive his garage of one access point, while the remaining access would be made narrower. In John's favour, one member of the Highways Committee was unhappy about the proposals as they considerably restricted movement to and from the garage. He thought there should be a measure of agreement between John Mitchell and the Town Council before any decision was made. It was also pointed out that the garage 'catered for all the buses on the island' and the proposed scheme would 'divert the highway clear of the garage.'

Less consideration to John Mitchell was made by another Councillor, who asked, 'What is Mr Mitchell motivated by – the amenity of the place, or his own petrol pump? At the back of his garage on Matheson Road, which is one of the beauty spots of Stornoway, there is what I consider a death trap – a bay where vehicles would be a danger to any child running along. I do not know how there have been no deaths there.' It is not obvious what relevance this had to the road improvement scheme – the matter of the open ramps was a separate matter between the Town Council and John Mitchell; perhaps, as in the past, it was a clash of personalities.

The matter of the garage boundary, pavements and parking of buses reared its head again shortly afterwards. On 18 July 1958, the Stornoway Gazette headline read, 'The Vanishing Footpath – Mystery at Mitchell's Garage.' The article related to a court case regarding where the road finished and the pavement began, which referred back to the conditions of the feu of 1936. Alan Mackenzie, a driver with John Mitchell, pleaded not guilty to parking a bus outside Mitchell's Garage on 5 April without lights, with the number plate unilluminated, and wilfully causing an obstruction by allowing the bus to overhang the pavement.

The crux of the case rested on the assumption by the defence that the division between John Mitchell's feu and the public footpath was not clearly defined. Mr D N Kesting, for the defence, maintained that over the years the tarmacadam from the road had clearly overlapped the

pavement, until it was no longer possible to say where each started and finished. Sheriff Campbell Ross commented, 'the whole question of this feu seems to have been mismanaged from the start. Having seen the place I cannot help knowing that it is very difficult to tell where the footpath is.'

Mr Colin Scott Mackenzie, Procurator Fiscal, remarked that, 'witnesses and the police seem to know where the division is and if Mr Mitchell and the accused don't know where it is after twenty years, it's high time they learned.' But John Mitchell said there was no way of telling where the road started or finished. When he had laid down the concrete on his feu and made the pavement twenty years ago there had been no tar on the road. He also said he had buses parked in front of his garage for the same length of time and no one had complained before.

Sheriff Ross commented that, 'the appropriate action should have been taken by the appropriate people. It should not have been allowed to drift on for years like this. It is fantastic.' There then followed a convoluted discussion on whether or not there was a kerb outside the garage. The next defence witness was Provost A J Mackenzie, who stated that he was a member of the Stornoway Trust when the feu for the garage site had originally been granted. He was asked if both the Town and County Councils had accepted the present position for some twenty years. 'No,' he replied, 'they have complained and protested repeatedly about the congestion.' He agreed he had been the person who had made the initial complaint. It was stated that there had been numerous other complaints from the public about the obstruction of the footpath.

Mr Kesting then asked the Dean of Guild why, in twenty years, no one had complained to John Mitchell. The response was, 'There may have been no complaints to the office, but Mr Mitchell is a difficult man to approach.' The Stornoway Gazette commented that John Mitchell, who was seated in the public benches, 'smiled broadly at this.'

Mr Kesting then alluded to the ill-feeling which had existed between John Mitchell and some of the Trustees. 'There has always been considerable strife over the granting of this feu in the first place, which is at the back of a lot of what has been heard here, rather than any complaint from the general public.' The Sheriff commented at this. 'This is certainly a tangled skein, but I don't think we need to go into that.' The outcome of this case was not reported in the Stornoway Gazette.

The Court was not finished yet with John Mitchell and complaints about parked vehicles. A further case was heard in March 1959, when

Parking of buses outside the garage on Matheson Road and Bayhead led to further brushes with the law.

John Mitchell was charged with causing vehicles to be parked longer than necessary, perhaps another situation which could have been diffused before reaching the Court, or which might again possibly have been brought out of ill-feeling against John Mitchell. As will be seen, on this occasion John Mitchell did not win his case, having presented a somewhat flimsy defence.

Two police constables, P.C. Mackenzie and P.C. Macleod, arrived at Matheson Road on 11 December 1958 at 11am and noted eight vehicles parked in a continuous line. One said, 'There were two Bedford lorries, five Bedford buses and a Vauxhall Velux car.' The police checked and found that they all belonged to Mitchell's Garage. They watched for about half-an-hour and saw that no-one had come to remove any of them. At this point they went to the garage, 'to see who had left them there.' The transport manager, Mr Mackenzie, explained that the garage had to be cleared out for the day's work, and it was understood that these vehicles had to go out to make room for working space.

John Mitchell questioned the policemen, who agreed that they had not seen who had parked the buses on the road. John suggested that whoever had parked the buses should have been charged, but P.C.

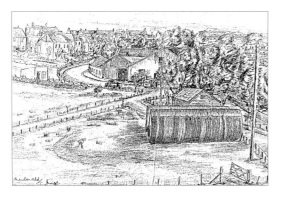

A drawing of the garage made in 1949. It shows the original buildings between Bayhead and Matheson Road. The open ground on the other side of Matheson Road, occupied only by the original premises of Charles Macleod, butchers, was the area that John unsuccessfully tried to obtain in the early 1940s. (Stornoway Historical Society)

The garage frontage on Bayhead in the 1960s.

Mackenzie started to explain why he had charged John Mitchell and not the driver of the buses. P.C. Mackenzie said the section under which Mitchell was charged said the person who allowed such an offence to take place was liable to be charged.

The policemen then stated that they had not spoken to John Mitchell at the time, but had pointed out the parked vehicles to John's transport manager.

The transport manager then said that the police had not shown him the vehicles parked on Matheson Road. Mackenzie then told the Burgh prosecutor that he had not seen eight vehicles parked on Matheson Road, but that he agreed that the garage was cleared for space for working. Summing up, the Burgh prosecutor said that it did not necessarily follow that the person who left the vehicles parked there was the guilty person. 'The police can charge the owner,' he said. 'They don't need to go chasing around to find the person. The owner must be responsible for what his employees do.'

Speaking on his own behalf, John Mitchell then criticised the way the case had been handled, saying there had been no evidence to show that the vehicles were actually there. He added, 'It was not brought to my notice on the 11th, to Mr Mackenzie's [the transport manager] notice or to anyone else's in my employment.' He then said that the Act he was charged under was dated as far back as 1892. This was the Burgh Police (Scotland) Act, Section 381, sub-section 10. 'In that time,' he said, 'there wasn't such a thing as a motor lorry or a bus.'

Garage staff in the 1960s. From left to right, Donald Maclennan (Dòmhnall Geal), Patsy (from New Valley), Rab Macmurdo, Murdo Maclennan (Gress), Norman Maclean (Ness), Murdo Maciver (Twist) and Donald Maciver (Billy Bones).

Staff in the 1960s taking time to relax: Alan Airidhbhruach, Toovie, Ina Matheson and Alex na Faochag.

Giving judgment, Baillie Stewart said that it had definitely been established that the vehicles were on Matheson Road. The police had approached the transport manager and 'he didn't appear sufficiently interested to go and see that there was a breach taking place.' Baillie Stewart concluded, 'I am satisfied that the case has been proven.'

As a result, John Mitchell was given the option of paying a fine of £1 or 10 days in prison. It must be assumed that he took the first option.

This would appear to have been the last skirmish in the long-running battle between John Mitchell and both the Stornoway Trust and the Town Council. It is not known if relations were improved in any way, but there were no further reports of any more court cases.

The Garage flourishes

The Garage flourished and expanded through the 1950s, particularly as car ownership began to steadily increase. More space became necessary and in 1960 John Mitchell bought the former Back Transport Ltd garage building in Back. This had originally been a hanger used during the Second World War as a seaplane base at Cuddy Point at Stornoway, so it was almost returned to its original location. With this additional space it became possible to complete the first purpose-built car showroom on the island.

The whole building took up the complete area from Bayhead Street to Matheson Road, roadside to roadside. There was a forecourt where the petrol pumps were located. On the Bayhead Street side it was split into distinct areas: there was the commercial vehicle area and heavy goods garage, and the bus garage which was on the Bayhead side of the building. In the centre was the section dealing with car repairs and on the left hand side looking in from Bayhead, on the Matheson Road side, was the body shop.

The Parts Department and the Showroom were in the same building with the entrance to them off Bayhead Street; the Parts Department counter was located at the back of the showroom. There was a retail counter and to feed the various workshops there was a small, square hatch facing out on to the garages, the staff would come there for materials. All records were kept manually, using pen and paper; there were no computers. When a job requiring parts came in, a job card was made out for that particular vehicle and the employee would come to the Parts Department for the material and the parts which would then be recorded on the back of the card. This was all done by the foreman.

Car Hire was dealt with in the office. This part of the business was strong as no other company was hiring on a similar scale. Almost all of the car hire clientele came from the mainland, mainly sales representatives coming to do business on the island. The customers would be collected from the airport and brought back to the garage to complete the paperwork before hiring a car for a few days.

The garage was one of the largest employers in Stornoway. In the mid-1960s there were about forty people employed, not including bus drivers for about twelve or fifteen buses. There were about six or seven working in the body shop and a similar number of mechanics, a couple of men working on bus repairs, and fifteen to twenty in the workshop. Three people worked in the Parts Department, there was one in sales, and another four or five people in the office. The petrol pump offices were separate, as they had to be open at night so the access to them was different; they had their own lockable door, and that's where the switchboard was to receive calls at night sometimes. Another three or four girls worked there as well as an apprentice selling petrol. The petrol pumps were open from 8 o'clock in the morning until 11 at night and therefore the staff had to work in shifts.

Stornoway Gazette 4 November 1960

MR MITCHELL'S MIDNIGHT VISITOR

On Monday night at 22.26pm a man broke a pane of glass in a window of Mitchell's Garage, Bayhead; at 12.45am next morning, Mr John Mitchell, 4 Sand Street, heard a sound outside his house and went downstairs to find the same man in his kitchen.

When the man involved appeared in Stornoway Sheriff Court on Tuesday he pled guilty to both the offences. He had, said Mr C. Scott Mackenzie, Procurator Fiscal, come up to Stornoway to see a girl and when he was disappointed in his reception had got drunk. When Mr Mitchell switched on the light in the garage after hearing the sound of breaking glass, he had gone away. Later, when Mr Mitchell found him inside his house, he said he wanted a bed for the night. It was a strange co-incidence that he should land at the house after having been at the garage, but he did not know Mr Mitchell, nor did Mr Mitchell know him. The accused, a motor mechanic from Old Kilpatrick, was fined £4.

Overleaf: An aerial view of the garage in the 1960s.

14. MEETING THE CHALLENGES OF RUNNING BUSES

During the late 1950s it was becoming clear to John Mitchell that operating bus services on Lewis, in common with the other operators on the island and throughout the British Isles, was becoming increasingly difficult. Making ends meet was becoming ever more challenging, passenger numbers on the country routes decreased and running costs steadily rose. The one bright spot was that as the population of Stornoway increased, so did the use of the town services. No new routes had been opened up in the rural areas, and some services had been curtailed. Even the summer excursions and tours were not covering their costs.

John Mitchell looked for ways to increase traffic and revenue. As an auxiliary service he introduced a service for collection and delivery of parcels to and from all the areas served by his company's buses. Delivery was usually made the same day as collection, and it cost less than by post for smaller items, while it was very convenient for transporting larger and heavier items to country districts. In many ways it was replacing the traditional system whereby these items had been casually carried on the buses, but which had been frowned upon by the Traffic Commissioners. The service was available for both the general public and local businesses.

In an effort to further the number of passengers carried John Mitchell made arrangements with travel agents to allow discount fares for visitors. He also believed that encouraging more visitors to come to Lewis would benefit the island as a whole, including to his own business. He advocated that this could be achieved with the provision of more accommodation, this being provided by both the island's hotels and by local inhabitants opening their doors for bed and breakfast accommodation,

Despite all the difficulties, in 1959 John Mitchell decided a bus station should be built at Stornoway. He considered that this would help to stimulate passenger business, and he also felt it right that he should provide proper facilities for all intending passengers. The Stornoway Gazette reported that there would be 'revolutionary improvements in conditions for Lewis bus passengers' when the Stornoway Harbour

Top: The typical buses of the 1960s onwards were Bedford OBs. Two are seen passing on a narrow country road.
Bottom: A typical scene at the bus station at the end of the day as passengers board buses for both town and country destinations.

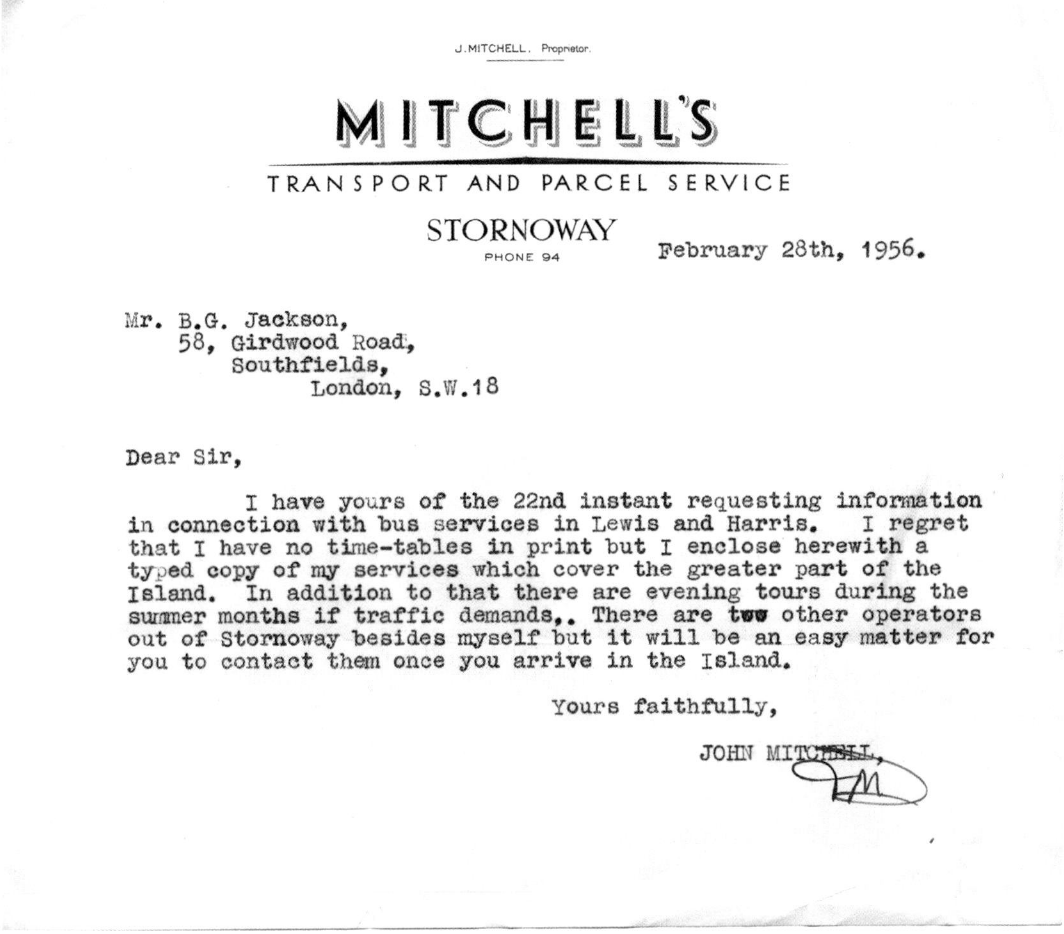

MITCHELL'S

TRANSPORT AND PARCEL SERVICE

STORNOWAY
PHONE 94

February 28th, 1956.

Mr. B.G. Jackson,
   58, Girdwood Road,
      Southfields,
         London, S.W.18

Dear Sir,

     I have yours of the 22nd instant requesting information in connection with bus services in Lewis and Harris. I regret that I have no time-tables in print but I enclose herewith a typed copy of my services which cover the greater part of the Island. In addition to that there are evening tours during the summer months if traffic demands.. There are two other operators out of Stornoway besides myself but it will be an easy matter for you to contact them once you arrive in the Island.

     Yours faithfully,

        JOHN MITCHELL,

No printed bus timetables were available in the 1950s
as this letter replying to a request for one shows.

Commission agreed to let John have the site of the former curing station on Cromwell Street quay. This area had been used as a scrap metal dump and it was considered very unlikely that it would ever be required as a curing station in the future.

John Mitchell's idea was to get the passengers under cover in weather-proof shelters while they were waiting for buses, which would travel along the quay and pick up their passengers from three bays. It was considered that this would be of particular benefit to people travelling on the longer journeys to Tolsta, Ness and Harris, who had often had to make their journeys in wet clothes after waiting in the rain and wind. He also intended to have offices, a parcel deposit centre and a transport information bureau all located in the building. The next step was to get the approval of the planning authority.

This was duly obtained, and although no financial assistance was forthcoming from the Town Council, the County Council, or from any other body, John Mitchell went ahead with his plan and the bus station was completed in the same year. The land was duly leased from the Stornoway Harbour Authority. As planned there were three bays for buses and a modern block with offices, a waiting room, toilets and a left-luggage department. Owing to its having previously been a curing station and its proximity to where fish had been landed for many years, the bus station became familiarly known as 'Billingsgate.'

In March 1960 the title of the bus company was altered from the now rather anachronistic Mitchell's Transport and Parcel Service to John Mitchell (Stornoway) Ltd. At the same time the bus company made its last purchase, buying Western Lewis Coaches Ltd. This last-mentioned concern had been formed in 1948 by the amalgamation of eight operators wishing to rationalise their services between Stornoway and the west side of Lewis, thereby avoiding unnecessary competition. It operated a West Side Circular service, and by taking it over another bit of competition was removed. Western Lewis Coaches retained its identity as it was operated as a subsidiary, although with the same directors as John Mitchell (Stornoway) Ltd, and all business was now run from Mitchell's office at 70 Bayhead Street, the official address of the garage. At the same time the opportunity was taken to paint the buses of both fleets in a new livery of dark blue with a cream stripe, replacing the light and royal blue of Mitchell and the green and cream of Western Lewis Coaches. There is no evidence as to why the two bus companies retained their individuality; it must be assumed that it was for business purposes.

Jessie Morrison: Memories of a conductress in the 1950s

I was 18 years old when I started as a conductress in the early 50s, and I often laugh thinking of when I went for an interview with Mr Mitchell (senior). I was so nervous I made my mother go with me! She made me wear my good suit, which was light blue and was normally kept just for going to church or weddings, etc.

Mr Mitchell was a big man, and I shook like a leaf when he asked us to come into the office where he gave us a seat. He was so tall and heavily built but he was a real gentleman and as I later found out, was very good to his staff. I also remember the day young Ian came in, and I thought, 'Oh what a smasher!' It was then I realised he was the son of Mr Mitchell.

There were no vacancies on the town runs but I was given a job on the Stornoway to Harris run – Kenny 'Keose' was the driver. Mr Mitchell showed me how the work was done. The machines had a disk with a hole for the fingers. The fares were 1 penny, 2d, 3d, and so on. We had to fill a compartment at the bottom of the machine and keep the roller full of ink, which was dark blue. There was also a thick felt pad to protect your clothes from this ink.

On the Harris run we took a lot of messages from shops, dropping off at different places whatever orders had to be delivered from the shops in town. This was a daily occurrence where we reached Rodel before returning home around 8 o'clock each night.

After a short time a vacancy came up on the town run and I was put on it, running from Melbost to Newmarket. My driver then was Kenny Martin, but as it was shift work we would have different drivers – it was the same for clippies.

Some of the staff were Kenny Martin (Parkend), Alex 'Faochag' Macleod, Dan (Plasterfield), Angie Maciver (Benside), and Donnie 'Buishie' (Melbost); also Nancy (Seaforth Rd), Sandra and Kirsty Smith 'Nogan' (Portona Drive) and Martha, who tragically died in a bus accident.

Ishbel and Ina worked in the offices and what a lot of pennies and halfpennies they counted each day. The conductresses' bags got so heavy with the money they had to empty them when their shoulders started aching with the weight!

May/August holidays were the highlight of the year, with every bus booked for trips to the beaches

Some of Mitchell's staff in the 1950s.
Top left: D A Macvicar and Ina Matheson. Top right: Kenny 'Keose' Macaulay and Sandra, from Tolsta.
Middle left: Norman Murray (Rasdie), Agnes Gillies (Ness), Ina Matheson and Murdani Macdonald.
Bottom left: Posing for the camera behind a bus on North Beach are Catriona Murray, Willie Logan,
Ian Aonghais Ghobha and an unknown conductress. Bottom right: A conductress from Ness.

Top: To provide better facilities for passengers the bus station on Cromwell Street Quay was opened in 1959.
This view shows the waiting room and office facilities.
Bottom: A Bedford of Western Lewis Coaches, later taken over by John Mitchell, waits for passengers on South Beach.
As well as the name of the owner written on the side of the bus, are the words 'Maximum speed 30 mph'.
It is unlikely that speed would be reached on many of the island roads in the 1950s.

Top: A winter scene at the bus station.
Bottom: In the late 1950s a parcel delivery service was introduced.

15. IAN MITCHELL TAKES THE REINS

Ian Mitchell was born in Stornoway on 13 December 1933. He was educated at The Nicolson Institute, the local secondary school. Ian did not take kindly to sitting at a desk with books in front of him, preferring to spend his time at his father's garage. Such was his antipathy to his education that Ian missed his final exams. His father John had offered to take Ian on a work trip to the mainland, not realising that this coincided with the exam dates, and Ian was only too pleased to go with his father. Ian later reported that his parents didn't speak to him about this offence, but the school made him repeat a year's classes, at the end of which, he again skipped his exams! This led to Ian spending time at a college in Glasgow, his parents probably trying to ensure that he obtained suitable qualifications. On leaving Glasgow he then commenced training to become a motor engineer, receiving his tuition both at Vauxhall Motors in Luton and at the Michigan plant of General Motors, Vauxhall's parent company, in the United States.

If traditional schooling was anathema to Ian, he clearly discovered his forte in the more practical engineering training. Without a doubt he was much more enthusiastic and hard-working, as comments on his Apprentice Report for August 1953 show. He had received four week's training in the machine shop, four weeks in the body shop and nine weeks in the trim shop. He had also taken courses in Workshop Trigonometry, Algebra and Clear Thinking. There was more to being a motor engineer than just knowing about engines and bodies! The section on practical work and progress reported that Ian 'got down to the practical side well, showed energy and interest in all operations,' that his 'conduct was beyond reproach,' and that he 'carefully observed all operations but did not work physically.' The accompanying letter to his father, from the Organizer – Dealer Executive Training, informed him that he was sure that John would 'be very gratified to read of his [son's] steady progress,' adding that he saw 'Ian occasionally and I must say he is turning out a well-built, healthy-looking lad.'

Top left: Ian Mitchell as a schoolboy. Top right: Ian – as a young man. Bottom left: John in contemplative mood.
Behind him are examples of the fruits of his labours: the garage, a bus and a Vauxhall car.
Bottom right: Ian in the garage office, after he had assumed the reins in the business.

Ian Mitchell returned to assist his father in the family business about 1954, when as well as continuing the bus operations he further developed the Vauxhall-Bedford Franchise which the company had held for many years. Like his father and grandfather before him, Ian was a Gaelic speaker, and he regularly spoke the language in his work.

In 1960 Ian Mitchell married Catherine Anne Bain, a member of a well-known and respected Stornoway family. Sadly their first child was stillborn, but in 1963 the couple became a family when a son, Christopher, was born. Anne was an active member of the community, volunteering for various charities and singing in the Stornoway Gaelic Choir; in addition, she worked occasionally in the garage office, and steadfastly supported Ian's career.

John Mitchell died suddenly on 14 March 1961. A fitting tribute to him appeared in the Stornoway Gazette issued on the following Thursday. Under the headline of 'Sudden Death of Garage Proprietor,' it read

> Mr John Mitchell, the Stornoway garage proprietor, died suddenly late on Tuesday night. He was on his way home, having closed the garage and taken some of his employees home, when he became ill at the wheel of his car close to the home of his son, Ian, on Matheson Road. He died almost at once.
>
> Mr Mitchell had built up over the years what, at the time of his death, was one of the largest privately owned transport businesses in the North of Scotland. The son of the late Mr and Mrs Donald Mitchell [also named George, as he was normally known], 22 South Shawbost, he served as a cavalry officer in the First World War. He was in his early twenties when he started the first bus service in Lewis, on a circular route from the town to Carloway and Barvas – a route which is still covered by his buses today. Later he managed the garage owned by Mr Maciver, his uncle, and in 1933 branched out on his own.
>
> Today, "Mitchell's" includes the largest garage on the island, a fleet of twenty-five buses, and a number of lorries and of cars for self-drive hire.
>
> The firm's buses serve the town, the west and north of Lewis, and do a daily run to Rodel, as well as special services all the year round and regular tours for visitors during the summer.
>
> When he first set up in business, his garage was on Esplanade Road, and it was three years before the site on which the

garage now stands, at the corner of Matheson Road and Bayhead, became his. Meantime there had been a spectacular dispute, which ended in the House of Lords. He was granted the corner feu in January, 1933 by Stornoway Trust, but the following month the site was withdrawn. Mr Mitchell took legal advice against the Trust in the Court of Session, where he was unsuccessful. When the case was taken to the House of Lords, however, the decision given in 1936 was in his favour.

He is survived by his wife, the former Christine Maclean of Bragar, by his son Ian, who assisted him in the business, and by his daughter, Chrissie, now Mrs Henry and married in Canada. Four of his brothers and sisters are alive; Norman is in Winnipeg, Donald is in Australia, Margaret Jean in Wyoming and Rachel in Glasgow.

With the unexpected passing of his father in 1961, Ian Mitchell took over the complete running of the garage, bus and quarry businesses. Ian said 'that a lot of people thought that I was born with the proverbial spoon in my mouth but the fact of the matter is that my old man dropped dead on Saturday night and I had a business to run on Monday and I knew very little about it.' Regrettably, Ian had not been told a great deal about the organisation and running of various parts of those businesses by his father, and although Ian felt he was not really prepared for the task, he assumed the mantle of Managing Director, continuing the development of the garage, and running the bus companies, but selling the quarry. John Mitchell had never intended that his son be involved in the quarry business, and although the quarry had initially been profitable in the 1950s, demand for quarried material had declined by the early 1960s once the construction of the local radar stations was complete.

A New Broom at the Garage

The change at the helm of the Garage became evident across the 1960s and 70s as Ian changed operations from his father's more informal and laid-back style to a modern business-like approach. No longer were things left until tomorrow, or payments made next month. A lot of the older generation on Lewis did not take too kindly to this change in attitude! This business approach included such things as recording all vehicles bought and sold (information which had not been kept previously), and a forty-six page Employee Handbook; this included information on company rules, the legal rights for the employees, health and safety (seventeen pages) and a section entitled 'When things go wrong.' Ian's foreword to the Handbook concluded by saying to his staff, 'I know that you can be relied upon to support this policy.'

It was clear that Ian planned not just to continue the success of the business, but to build on it. The staff were now organised in a three-level structure, with four supervisors – dealing with finance, new and used vehicles, servicing and parts – working below the Managing Director, and teams of operatives in each section reporting to their respective Supervisor.

Ian Mitchell became a member of the Institute of the Motor Industry and the institute of Directors, now known as the Chartered Management Institute. In 1968 he graduated from a Vauxhall Motors Dealer Management Seminar and in 1972 successfully attended a Dealer Standard Accounting course at Luton.

Ian Mitchell had further expanded the business during the late 1960s. A Massey-Ferguson franchise was added, with both tractors and other farming equipment being advertised for sale, and the garage became the local agency for Michelin Tyres. Fiat and Opel agencies were added during the 1970s. Mitchell's also operated a driving school, with testers visiting the island every few months to examine a batch of learner drivers.

Perhaps realising that training to work in the motor industry could not begin early enough, Ian Mitchell was involved in a careers convention held in the Nicolson Institute in March 1969, taking the opportunity to present to Edward Young, Rector of the school, two fully equipped engines which had been part of Mitchell's convention display; the engines were to be used by the school's technical department. This commitment to youth and training was further exemplified in 1978 when Ian Mitchell became involved with a visit of the Road Transport Industry Training Board which made a visit to Stornoway to discuss the setting up of a new motor vehicle integrated course at Lews Castle Technical College.

Car Sales

Selling both new and used cars was an important part of the business. As mentioned above, franchises with leading manufacturers were gradually obtained, with the Bedford-Vauxhall connection always being to the fore. Gradually over the years the number of dealerships declined – it went down to Vauxhall, Bedford, Fiat and Volkswagen; then Fiat and Volkswagen went, probably because these companies did not want their product running alongside another one. Bedford and Vauxhall remained until the end.

The Car Sales department was run by 'Jimsie' Afrin, who was still working for the Mitchells since he started from school in 1927. He was

Top: Inside the modernised garage: the Parts Department seen through 'the hatch'.
Bottom: Ian is seen here graduating from a Vauxhall Motors Dealer management seminar.

Ian, seen here second left in the front row, attended management seminars to broaden his knowledge of the trade.

allowed almost total oversight of this aspect of the business, from the control of new stock to deciding what he would give for a used car coming in.

New vehicles came to the island on the mail boat, the *Loch Seaforth*. This was before the days of 'drive-on-drive-off' ferries. All the vehicles had to be loaded on to the ship at Kyle of Lochalsh by crane, with nets beneath the wheels and sacking to prevent scratching, being unloaded at Stornoway by the same procedure. A unique method of bringing the cars to Stornoway would often be used. Ian Mitchell had a number of contacts, either someone working on the mainland or a merchant seaman coming home on leave. These people would phone Ian and ask, 'Any cars to come up the road from Glasgow?' and he might reply, 'Yes, there's a Vauxhall Victor at SMT.' They would collect the car and drive it up to be loaded on the steamer at Kyle of Lochalsh, with Ian paying the ferry fare. There were also occasions when there were maybe eight or nine new cars ordered for stock, and Kenny 'Keose' and 'Jimsie' Afrin would go off to the mainland for a week with trade plates. They would travel to Glasgow by train and pick two cars up, come back up the road and leave the cars at Kyle of Lochalsh, then hitch a lift back to Glasgow and bring more cars up, staying in hotels overnight. On their return, the garage would echo to stories of their near escapes coming through places such as Drumochter in winter in the snow.

The new cars arrived with a coating of protective wax on them. It was part of the job of an apprentice to remove this wax. This was far from an easy task as in those days there were none of the detergents and additives which are available today. The apprentice was supplied with an enamel pail with paraffin in it and a rag. Great care had to be taken not to scratch the new paintwork, and with the job having to be done between serving petrol it could sometimes take a day to do one car. The cars also came without the carpets fitted in them, these being stored in the boot, and they, too, had to be fitted. Petrol was cheap at that time, 4/5d and 4/9d a gallon; it was cheap enough that new cars would be sold with a full tank.

Second hand cars came in as trade-ins; if they were in good condition an effort would be made to tidy them up – 'Jimsie' Afrin was expert at renovating cars – before reselling them. If a trade-in was in very poor condition, it might be sold off for as little as a fiver.

Other employees could help in selling a car. If 'Jimsie' Afrin was involved in something else and an employee happened to be in the car showroom that person would 'hang on' to the prospective customer, chatting to them and showing them a car. If they subsequently bought a car the 'salesman' would be given a monetary reward.

The Garage is rebuilt

In 1971 Ian Mitchell submitted plans for replacing the existing petrol storage tanks with new ones. Planning permission was obtained from Ross and Cromarty County Council in June 1971, followed one month later by a building warrant from Stornoway Town Council. The work was carried out by William Tawse Ltd, a local contractor. By 1 December the old tank had been steamed clean and was then removed. Construction of the new tanks did not prove to be straightforward; a great deal of difficulty was incurred during the excavation for the first new tank, due to extreme pressure of water and tidal conditions. It was considered that the only way of fitting the new tank was to partially fill it with water prior to concreting the surround. This was the only method which could be used to ensure that the buoyancy of the tank would not cause it to tear out the anchors from the base concrete. All three tanks were finally installed by 16 December.

Overleaf: Part of a display held at 'the Acres' in Stornoway to demonstrate the wide variety of vehicles and agricultural machinery that was sold.

In 1973, further development of the buildings took place, the work being carried out by a local contactor, Willie Macleod, known locally as 'Willie Bucach'. The original premises were demolished, to be replaced by a new garage with office block and a covered petrol forecourt. The garage was now in its final state. The main showroom, for displaying new cars, was a modern rectangular single storey building fronting on to Bayhead with an office suite to the left and a concrete forecourt. At the rear of the main showroom, with access from Matheson Road, was the Parts Department warehouse and a large workshop area. This was designed for servicing commercial vehicles and buses as well as cars. There was a paint workshop at the rear of this area. Bordering on both Matheson Road and Bayhead Street was a large concrete parking area. All the floor levels were raised by one metre during reconstruction; this was done as historically it had been shown that the area was subject to flooding during extremely wet weather. The whole area, both buildings and forecourt, had also been underlain with high quality aggregate designed to withstand use by heavy commercial vehicles. The floor was painted red with yellow lines and marked out in bays. The old pits in which men had previously worked beneath vehicles were replaced with hydraulic ramps.

It took eighteen months to complete the modernisation and reorganisation. All involved Ian Mitchell in working long hours. He would be there in the morning at nine and he would be there when the last bus came in at eleven. Eventually, he received a warning from his doctor that he was working too much and that his health was at serious risk. Ian did cut back on his working hours, and took up golf as a form of relaxation.

However, to let the island people know he was back in business Ian Mitchell organised a Grand Opening Night. The event was reported on the front page of Vauxhall-Bedford News published at the time.

> Friends from up to sixty miles away were among more than 250 well-wishers at Ian Mitchell's Grand Opening Night.
>
> It was an impressive display he put on with several new Vauxhalls, on ramps so that their undersides could be inspected, and a rolled-over Viva with mirrors and labels pointing to product features.
>
> A selection of used cars was also on show and engine tune demonstrations were given during the evening.

Top: In relaxed mood in the Garage are: back row, Donald Morrison (Tarag), Donald Martin, Angus Macdonald, Ian 'an Tony and Jimmy 'Blake' Maciver; front row, Ian 'Barvas' Maciver, Ivor Maclean, Colin Macritchie, Murdo John Mackenzie, Finlay Mackenzie and John Sinclair. Bottom: In March 1969 Ian donated two fully equipped engines to The Nicolson Institute for use in the school's technical department. He is seen here handing them over to Edward Young, the school's Rector.

Top: The garage, looking towards Bayhead.
Bottom: An aerial view of the garage after its expansion in the late 1960s.
Opposite: Advertisements published in the Stornoway Gazette during the 1960s.

The Mini Theatre, mounted in the back of a Bedford Double Plus, was an unending attraction – 'the first time we've seen colour television on Lewis', one guest commented.

A hole-in-one contest in the workshop drew many entries; so – with the lure of a bottle of whisky as the prize – did a How Many Balloons in a Viva? Competition.

Following the reception Ian invited sixty customers to a Ceilidh (a Highland party) which finished at two o'clock the next morning.

A second evening event – which, like the opening reception, attracted press coverage – was a pie-eating contest.

Ian leafed through his file of *V-B News* and noting stories of successful bean-eating and similar events, decided on a pie-eating contest using the traditional Scottish meat pie.

Wretched weather limited the number of contestants but a band of fifty supporters turned out to cheer them on.

Demolishing the opposition – and ten pies – was 15-year-old Kenneth Dingwall. After he'd put away his ninth pie Kenneth was looking decidedly queasy as his fans urged him to carry on and his mother urged him to stop!

Throughout the week Ian advertised special offers:

- On all cash sales over £2, a pair of tights for women customers and a car sponge for the men.
- Free fitting of all V-B accessories.
- Free winter safety check on any make of vehicle.
- Radio fitted to every new car; and a portable radio with every used car.

It is too early yet to judge the effect of what was, for the most part, a public relations exercise, but Ian reports two new cars sold already and more in the pipeline.

Top: The car showroom. Bottom: Advertising the Triumph Herald in the 1960s.
Overleaf: A relaxed Ian stands with some of his staff. From left to right: Ian Mitchell, Calum Macdiarmid, Jimsie Afrin, Ruairidh (Tolsta), Alan Airidhbhruach, Dan Macinnes, Davie Macfarlane, John Macinnes (Swede), Donnie Mackenzie, John Graham, Alistair Beaton and unknown.

16. DECLINE OF THE BUSES

Following the death of his father in 1961, Ian Mitchell took over the running of the bus companies. The first action taken by Ian Mitchell took place on 12 May 1961, when a long established tradition involving the running of Mitchell's buses came to an end. This was the custom of the buses finishing their journey by travelling along Cromwell Street Quay from the sloping, curved entrance at Bayhead. This route had been used from the earliest days, and buses continued to end their journeys the same way after the bus station had been opened in 1959. On a number of occasions in icy or very wet conditions, buses had almost fallen into the Inner Harbour when turning on to the quay.

In the winter of 1959 Baillie Mrs Urquhart had raised the question at a meeting of Stornoway Town Council of Mitchell's Buses carrying passengers along Cromwell Street Quay. She said that 'her heart was in her mouth when she had to travel along the snow-and ice-covered pier in a heavy bus,' adding, 'It was extremely dangerous.'

After unsuccessfully asking Mr Mitchell to reroute his buses, the Council wrote a letter to the Traffic Commission regarding the matter. The reply was read to the Council at their meeting in May 1960. Mr Robertson, the Commissioner, wrote that he could not take any action as long as the police objected to the alternative route, taking buses along Cromwell Street. He suggested adding an extra stop on Bayhead Street before the buses turned on to the quay, thus not requiring passengers to travel along the Quay. Mrs Urquhart was far from satisfied with this response, describing the Commissioner's attitude as 'absolutely high-handed.'

'It seems,' said Mrs Urquhart, 'that what the Traffic Commissioners are concerned with is what is suitable to them and to Mr Mitchell. It is not the feeling of those using the buses. I think it is absolutely high-handed of them to write such a letter. Has this man travelled on the bus? Has he come along the quay in snow and ice? I think that we must do something further about this. They are just imposing this on us.'

She remarked that she travelled on this route as much as anybody in town, and knew what the views of those travelling with her were. She gave a vivid description of how the turn on to the quay appeared

A familiar sight on the island in the 1960s. Buses were kept overnight at their destinations in the outlying villages, and could be seen parked as here, beside the driver's peat stack.

to the passenger, how the front of the bus was almost over the edge of the quay, adding, 'If there is the slightest error of judgement or the slightest ice on the road the bus could go over the edge.' It was agreed by the Council that the matter should be referred again to the Traffic Commissioners.

A formal objection to the routing was thus made at the meeting of the Traffic Commissioners sitting at Stornoway on Friday, 12 May 1961. On the grounds of passenger safety, the Traffic Commissioners fixed a new terminus of the route from Plasterfield, and services arriving from the country. This was at 27 North Beach Street; this meant buses would travel along Cromwell Street to the new terminus, after which they would proceed empty to the bus station. An alternative proposal for a new entrance from Cromwell Street just north of the bus station had to be dropped, as neither Ian Mitchell, who had made the application for this, nor the Harbour Commission, which was also involved, could agree as to who should bear the cost in services.

Initially, Ian continued to run the services of the two bus companies as before. The services for which licences were held can be separated into three groups. The first two were operated by John Mitchell (Stornoway) Ltd. The town services ran from Cromwell Street to

Overleaf: Buses wait on Cromwell Street Quay.

Melbost (approximately 2.5 miles), Marybank (3 miles), Plasterfield (2 miles) and to Laxdale (2 miles). There were five services to outlying areas; these ran to Tong and Back (7 miles), Tong, Back and Tolsta (14 miles), Ness (30 miles), to Tarbert (37.5 miles) and to Rodel and Leverburgh (64 miles). Western Lewis Coaches held a licence to operate the circular service from Stornoway to Barvas, Carloway and Callanish, a distance of 48 miles.

The table below indicates the approximate total mileage travelled on each route, along with the revenue, based on the year ending 31 March 1962.

Services	Mileage	Revenue (£)
Town services		
Laxdale	41,194	2,975
Melbost	43,205	3,085
Marybank	41,194	3,085
Plasterfield	33,949	2,975
	159,542	12,120
Back & Tong	90,986	7,676
Tolsta	71,023	8,071
	162,009	15,749
Ness	84,196	6,427
Tarbert, Rodel & Leverburgh	162,113	9,916
West Coast Circular	103,218	7,058
Total	671,078	51,270

The four town services required two buses, with four drivers and conductors, with an additional two to four vehicles at the lunch time peak hour. This fitted conveniently with the contract to serve BEA at the airport, which operated from approximately 11.00 to 12.00 and from 2.00 to 3.00, allowing the duplicate buses and crews to be fully utilised.

Tolsta and Back were served by four or five buses per day; this included school contracts, for which the Council paid £5,113 per year. There were also some shorter runs to Tong and Back, which, if combined with the Tolsta buses, could be more economical.

Two runs were made daily in each direction on the Ness service, with an additional third run each day except Wednesdays. If required, a special early morning run was offered on Mondays; it was required three Mondays out of four.

The Harris service required two buses during the winter months and four in summer. With about half of the not inconsiderable mileage

Mitchell's & Western Lewis Coaches Ltd.
Time Table, 1966

NESS DISTRICT
Daily except Wednesday and Monday during school terms :
Leave Ness .... 9.00 a.m.　　Arrive Stornoway ...... 10.30 a.m.
　　　　　　　　2.00 p.m.　　　　　　　　　　　　3.30 p.m.

Monday only during school terms :
Leave Ness .... 7.30 a.m.　　Arrive Stornoway ...... 8.45 a.m.
　　　　　　　　2.00 p.m.　　　　　　　　　　　　3.30 p.m.

Daily except Wednesday :
Leave Stornoway ...... 12.30 p.m.　　Arrive Ness .... 2.00 p.m.
　　　　　　　　5.45 p.m.　　　　　　　　　　　　7.15 p.m.

TOLSTA DISTRICT
Daily :
Leave Tolsta　7.00 a.m. (Ex. Sat.)　Arrive Sty.　7.45 a.m. (Ex. Sat.)
　　　　　　9.15 a.m.　　　　　　　　　　　　10.00 a.m.
　　　　　　2.00 p.m.　　　　　　　　　　　　2.45 p.m.
Leave Sty.　8.00 a.m. (Ex. Sat.)　Arrive Tolsta　8.45 a.m. (Ex. Sat.)
　　　　　　1.00 p.m.　　　　　　　　　　　　1.45 p.m.
　　　　　　6.10 p.m.　　　　　　　　　　　　6.55 p.m.

Friday Only :
Leave Tolsta .... 7.00 p.m.　　Arrive Stornoway ...... 7.45 p.m.
Leave Stornoway ...... 10.45 p.m.　　Arrive Tolsta .... 11.30 p.m.

WEST SIDE
Daily except Wednesday and Monday during school terms :
Leave Brue .... 9.00 a.m.　　Arrive Stornoway ...... 10.30 a.m.
(via Carloway)
Leave Stornoway ...... 12.30 p.m.　　Arrive Stornoway ...... 2.45 p.m.
(Circular)
Leave Stornoway ...... 5.30 p.m.　　Arrive Brue .... 7.00 p.m.
(via Carloway)

Monday only during school terms :
Leave Brue .... 7.30 a.m.　　Arrive Stornoway ...... 8.45 a.m.
(via Carloway)
Leave Stornoway ...... 12.30 p.m.　　Arrive Stornoway ...... 2.45 p.m.
(Circular)
Leave Stornoway ...... 5.30 p.m.　　Arrive Brue .... 7.00 p.m.
(via Carloway)

The 12.30 bus calls at Callanish Stones for the benefit of tourists, if desired.

TOWN SERVICE
Early morning runs from Laxdale, Melbost and Plasterfield and then :
LAXDALE : Hourly runs from Stornoway : 10.00 a.m. to 11.00 p.m.
MELBOST : Hourly runs from Stornoway : 9.00 a.m. to 11.00 p.m.
MARYBANK : Hourly runs from Stornoway : 9.30 a.m. to 10.30 p.m.
PLASTERFIELD : Hourly runs from Stornoway : 9.30 a.m. to 10.30 p.m.

The 1966 bus timetable.

Tarbert in the 1970s. By this time Mitchell's no longer operated the Harris service; it had been sold to John Morrison of Northton who in turn had sold the service to Highland Omnibuses. Two of their buses were on service to Rodel and Stornoway, while the third was a spare vehicle. The Mitchell's bus on the right was in Tarbert on a private hire.

being between Tarbert and Leverburgh the revenue from this section was small and not economic. A consideration was to reduce the service to three days per week, to coincide with the steamer calls (the mail ship from Mallaig and Kyle of Lochalsh only served Tarbert three times per week), but it was thought that the situation might change with the introduction of a car ferry to Harris in 1964, with more calls each week and probably more passengers.

The most uneconomic service was the West Side Circular. It only served a few villages and for much of the route – nine miles from Stornoway to Barvas and ten miles between Stornoway and Callanish – the land was virtually uninhabited.

In addition to the income from these services, Ian Mitchell had a number of separate contracts which supplemented his revenue. The school contract and that for BEA to the airport have been mentioned. There was also one post office contract. This was to carry mails between Stornoway and Carnish, about two or three bags per day. The annual revenue for this was £132. Ian Mitchell had also negotiated with SPD (a mainland delivery company) and Birds Eye to deliver packaged goods landed at Stornoway on the mail steamer. Most of this traffic was in Stornoway.

Up until 1963 the companies showed a reasonable profit and a satisfactory return on the capital employed. From then on the bus operations started to decline, with a corresponding decrease in revenue. Ways had to be sought to operate all the services as efficiently as possible, but it was difficult to see what economies could be introduced, other than those mentioned above.

Mairi Mackenzie: memories of a conductress in the 1960s

I started going on the bus with my mother when I was about three or four, and I remember taking the money from people, that's my earliest memories, is taking the fares from the people, walking up with my mother and taking the money and putting it in the bag and she would give me the ticket and I would give it to them.

My mother, who was then working in Woolworths, had been asked by John Mitchell if she would like to come and act as a nanny for his children. This she did, and she looked after Ian and his sister until Ian was almost school age.

John Mitchell then said he was planning to take on a conductress; would my mother like the job? So off she went and became a conductress and she was there from the time she was eighteen or nineteen until the time she got married, and then I arrived nine months later, so she didn't have much time then. When my father was in the War she went back and she was on the buses then until I was fifteen. Then she went back again and she was there until she was sixty. She was a long time with them.

She was a nice conductress compared to some, people used to say that; others tended to throw them off the bus when they were drunk. I remember her telling us one story about a fellow from Newmarket, there was something wrong with him, and he was in the Paratroopers and when he came back home he was on the bus and refused to pay his fare, so my mother said, 'Now, come on, come on, you're going to have to pay like everybody else.' The next thing he drew out this dagger and was really quite vicious about it and said, 'I could do a lot of damage to you with this.' So the bus was stopped and with help from the police he was thrown off the bus. That frightened her, but she stuck to it.

Now when I went on it was 1960; I'd come back from England and wanted a job for a couple of years and it was good, it was really good. I didn't get an interview – my mother just said to Ian Mitchell, 'Mairi's home, she's looking for a job,' and I was taken on. I think there was another conductress leaving at the time so it was just luck, I was there at the right time. I think John Mitchell was there for a wee while, but it was more Ian, he had taken over by then, he was running the show – his father may have been ill.

The days on the buses were good. What I remember most was men coming with fish, cod, huge things, their whole hand inside the head of this fish, trailing it up the bus, just trailing it, and then, of course, all the cailleachs were shouting, 'Watch my clothes, watch my clothes,' and the fish would be getting slapped all over the place, or the herring

Top: In icy or wet conditions driving on to Cromwell Street Quay could lead to accidents, such as shown here. This led to buses being re-routed to a new terminus on North Beach Street. Bottom: The new terminus, outside Alec Macaulay's drapers' shop on North Beach Street. This is still the main stop for all buses today.

on a piece of string, and they would put it on the floor, and then, of course, the floor was all streaky. This was going home, they would be just off a boat.

I was wearing stiletto heels, would you believe, up and down the bus with stiletto heels – stylish, yes. I started on the Marybank-Sandwick route, but then I said I wanted to go on to the Laxdale-Plasterfield one, because I lived on Nicolson Road, that was my run. You started one morning at eleven in the morning and then you didn't finish until eleven at night and the next day you would start at half past seven in the morning but then you finished at five o'clock, that was it, day about. I was never on the country run, they had their own conductresses and they were quite happy with that. The buses would stop at the driver's house at the end of the day. The driver that I had, old Dan, he was lovely, 'Shaky' Dan, he would stop at every house on the way out to Laxdale to let people off, every house he stopped at, with the result we would be running late. Then, of course, what would happen but Ian Mitchell would come charging like a bull: 'What are you running late for?'

In the morning the bus just picked me up at the corner at about a quarter to eleven and then got off here at night because my driver, old Dan, he was from Plasterfield and he took the bus home. When you came back from Laxdale at eleven o'clock you had to go into the office [to hand in the takings] but you tried to count the money before that so that when you went into the office everything was counted and you hoped it was going to work; you hoped it would – it was never over, I can assure you, it was never over, it was always under. At the end you pressed this button [on the ticket machine] and the whole total would come out, because every time you gave a ticket, whether it was twopence or fourpence or whatever, it registered this, so that at the end you clicked this little thing over so that the next thing that came out gave you the whole total that should have been in your bag. The money was never over, it was always out. I never helped myself [to money] but some of the drivers, and there was one especially, before you knew it, would help themselves to some extra cash and you kept your eye out when you knew it was nine o'clock and you would get to town.

Some of the drivers, they used to go for a pint on a Friday and a Saturday night, at nine o'clock they'd all be over at the pub. You really had to watch your bag because the drivers would put their hands into it for your money, with the result that you were short. And it was always the conductresses that got into trouble from Ian Mitchell about it, but you didn't dare say anything.

BACK DISTRICT

Leave Back		Arrive Stornoway	
	7.20 a.m.		7.40 a.m.
	8.20 a.m.		8 40 a.m.
	11.00 a.m.		11.20 a.m.
	4.00 p.m.		4.20 p.m.
	5.00 p.m.		5.20 p.m.
	7.20 p.m.		7.40 p.m.
	10.00 p.m.		10.20 p.m.
Leave Stornoway	8.00 a.m.	Arrive in Back	8.20 a.m.
	9.00 a.m.		9.20 a.m.
	11.30 a.m.		11.50 a.m.
	4.30 p.m.		4.50 p.m.
	5.30 p.m.		5.50 p.m.
	6.10 p.m.		6.30 p.m.
	9.30 p.m.		9.50 p.m.
	11.00 p.m.		11.20 p.m.

TONG DISTRICT

Leave Tong		Arrive Stornoway	
	7.30 a.m.		7.50 a.m.
	8.30 a.m.		8.50 a.m.
Leave Stornoway	6.10 p.m.	Arrive Tong	6.30 p.m.

Top left: A group of bus drivers in 1960: left to right, Dan Tong, Paddy Mackay, Donnie Fido and Angie Gay.
Top right: Mairi Mackenzie, a clippie in the 1960s. 'Would you believe, I was up and down the bus wearing stiletto heels – very stylish!' Bottom left: Mitchell's first clippie, Aggie Mackenzie, stands beside a bus with an unknown passenger.
Bottom right: Part of the 1966 timetable, showing services to the Back district.

On a Saturday night it was a riot, because then men would go down (into Stornoway) for a drink and later on they would be on the bus going home and, oh my goodness, it would be a riot. But not many fights, but there were a few fights when my mother was on the Laxdale run.

I remember old Shaky Dan, he was lovely, but at New Year, at every house in Laxdale, of course there weren't as many houses as there are now, old Dan would be in for a glass of whisky and it wasn't just a wee nip, and by the time we got back to town, I don't know how he kept his job because they must have realised.

The buses – I don't know how we ever survived because the bus drivers would be half sozzled , then everybody would pile on to the bus, there was no numbers, they all piled on. The driver would be sitting like that, all hunched up, trying to see where he was going, and all the people falling on top of him. And they were drunk as well, how we survived I don't know. There wasn't half the traffic, but the roads were narrower; a few times we were off the road, especially out at the end of Laxdale. If you went off the road there – I remember having to walk from right at the end of Newmarket all the way down to the first kiosk at the school, to phone the garage for somebody to come and help us; but you took it all in your stride.

Some buses, the ones with the engines inside, the fumes, I don't know how we didn't end up being killed. One of the drivers, he was on the way out to Laxdale and the driver had kept complaining, he was coughing a lot, and the fumes that night were dreadful and he said, 'That's it, I'm going into the office on the way back', so this was on the way back at eleven o'clock, I went in to put the money in and he went behind me and I heard him talking to Ian and then I heard the voices being raised a bit and I thought, 'Gosh, what's going on here?'. Anyway, I went back out to the bus, the driver came out and he said, 'You'll never believe this, Mairi, but I've just been given my books.' I said, 'Have you? Who by?' 'Ian Mitchell,' he said, 'because I complained about the fumes and said I wasn't driving that bus any more.' 'Well if you don't like it you can lump it.' And that was it finished – that was the driver gone, which you could do in those days, bosses could do that.

Ian Mitchell was always there at night to count the money. And if the money was short, oh dear. I was quite happy if my mother was on the other run, the Melbost-Marybank run, so sometimes we met in the office if she was there, and a few times she was there when Ian was having a go at me about the money. Well she had known, I'd been saying to her about the drivers taking money, and she was saying,

'Well you're just going to have to make it up with your own money,' and I said, 'No, I don't see why I should.' So I was at this set-to with Ian and my mother would come, and she was tall and her and Ian got on very well and Ian would back down if she gave him a telling off.

One time at the bus station one of the local characters had a mouth organ and they started playing it in the bus station and the conductresses Polly and my mother doing an eightsome reel – you wouldn't see that now.

There was a fellow up in Plasterfield, a shepherd he was, he tried to come on with a sheep one day but no he wasn't allowed. Dan said, 'No, you're not coming on.' Probably my mother would have let him.

Some memories of Ian

Ian was always doing things like coming out to the end of Laxdale where the bus stopped and coming in and checking – at the end of every run you had to work out how many tickets you had sold – he was always coming and checking this slip which we had, and just checking things. He really was quite awkward.

I remember meeting him many years later and he said, 'you know, I have to apologise to you for so many things that happened to you when you were a conductress, and it prays on my mind.' He and I had a love-hate relationship – I was very jealous of my mother and these children – he and his sister were very close to my mother.

Ian could really get quite hot about things. If the bus broke down it was as if it was the driver's fault, and that happened quite a lot. When the truck would come to give us a hand, he would follow in his own car, saying, 'What's going on here?' There was one time when the bus broke down at Plasterfield and old Dan was sitting there saying, 'I don't know what to do,' and the phone box up there was broken. So I walked all the way to Goathill Road, there was a phone box there, and then I walked all the way back – this was about ten o'clock at night – and when I got back Ian was there, and he said, 'What do you think you're doing here?' and I said, 'Well, I've just come back from the phone box.' 'Well, you can clear off now,' he said, 'You're not needed.' So I had to walk all the way home from Plasterfield.

Top left: From left to right: unknown, Chrissie, Aggie Mackenzie and Dòmhnall Atchy.

Top right: Drivers and conductresses in the 1960s. From left to right: Dan, Aggie, Paddy Mackay, Polly and Alec.

Bottom left: Buses to the country districts would wait for the arrival of the mail boat. This evocative picture shows the bus for Ness beside the *Loch Seaforth*, with bales of wool and the Harbour Authority's cranes in the background.

Bottom right: Ness conductresses. Overleaf: Parcels are being collected from the Harris bus at Leverburgh in the early 1960s.

An offer to David MacBrayne Ltd

In the light of the above precarious economic situation, and appreciating that as car ownership on the islands was increasing, the demand for bus services would equivalently decline, Ian Mitchell attempted in 1963 to sell the company's bus services to David MacBrayne Ltd, who already operated services in Harris and the Uists.

In their response to Ian Mitchell, David MacBrayne Ltd intimated that any prospective purchaser would be faced with considerable capital expenditure, particularly as the only assets included in the sale were the vehicles and the Bus Station in Stornoway. The latter was not an attractive proposition as it had been built on Harbour Commission ground on a three month lease; it was not considered worthwhile unless a long term lease were to be granted.

Twenty vehicles were offered for sale, thirteen of which were more than four years old. All were considered to be of the utility type, which MacBraynes considered to be satisfactory for town services and school runs, but they would have wished to run a 'more comfortable type of vehicle' on the longer services to Harris and Ness, a type which could also be used to develop tours and excursions. They considered that only ten of the vehicles would be suitable; the value of the other vehicles ranged between £50 and £800.

Although the revenue in 1963 was satisfactory, the prospective purchasers were aware that it was probable that income would decrease. There was little in the way of savings that could be made in the running of the services. Amalgamating the town services could save little, the Tolsta and Back services could be reduced, requiring fewer buses and staff, while the Ness, Harris and West Side runs were all running at basic levels.

It was estimated that to take over the services and operate them efficiently would require considerable capital expenditure, in addition to the purchase of the business. Garages would be required at Stornoway, Ness and Rodel, there were repair costs, and expenditure of about £14,000 was needed to purchase new vehicles for immediate use. The minimum outlay was considered to be between £20,000 and £30,000.

In the light of all these considerations it is perhaps not surprising that David MacBrayne Ltd declined to take up the offer.

In January 1974 a combination of a very high tide and a south-westerly gale led to flooding in Stornoway. Here one of Mitchell's buses pushes its way along a very watery South Beach Street.

A gradual reduction in services

With the offer to David MacBrayne Ltd having been declined, and no prospect of any improvement in the financial situation, Ian took steps to reduce both the services and the buses required to operate them. Fourteen vehicles were withdrawn between 1964 and 1965. In the latter year, John Morrison, of Northton in Harris, who had been operating services on that island since 1936, took over the two Stornoway-Harris services.

For operational reasons, the services to Ness and North Tolsta were transferred to Western Lewis Coaches. John Mitchell (Stornoway) Ltd now only operated two services, both being local runs in Stornoway. The fleet of John Mitchell (Stornoway) Ltd was reduced to only three in 1969 (and only one in the 1970s), with the others being transferred to the Western Lewis fleet, which numbered nine and eleven.

Not only was there a decline in passenger numbers but fuel costs rose steadily. As a result in 1964 a public inquiry was held to discuss the implications of applications by John Mitchell (Stornoway) Ltd and Western Lewis Coaches Ltd to withdraw their services catering for passengers coming off the mail boat at Stornoway each evening and travelling to North Tolsta, to Ness and to the West Side. Ian Mitchell represented both companies at the meeting with the Traffic Commissioners, and said that none of the services was paying, and that the revenue was not covering the cost of the fuel used, let alone the drivers' wages. The Tolsta run had an average of two or three passengers and sometimes none at all. After discussion it was agreed that the Tolsta service be discontinued, while the Ness service would operate only during the summer. The reduced services continued to operate on throughout the 1960s and 70s with little change. Arguments with the Traffic Commissioners appeared to have become a thing of the past, as had disputes with the local Council.

There was a disagreement of a different kind in March 1973 when twelve drivers went on strike. This affected all eight services, to Melbost, Laxdale, Marybank, Plasterfield, Back, Tolsta, the West Side and to Ness. The dispute arose over a new rate of pay, which the drivers claimed was not being paid to them. The secretary of the Transport and General Workers Union explained, 'The basic rate for drivers was increased last October to £21.56 per week and the drivers employed by Messrs Mitchell's are getting only £21 per week and want the 56p backdated to bring them into line with the national agreement.' The strike lasted a week, after which the drivers returned to work following an agreement being reached that the 56p would be paid and back-dated to the previous October. It should be mentioned that although the strike extended over a weekend the drivers did turn out voluntarily on the Sunday to take people to church.

In April 1976 one of Mitchell's buses and a car collided at the junction of Seaforth Road and Oliver's Brae. Two men died and a third was injured in the accident.

Two unhappy incidents

Two unhappy incidents involved Mitchell's buses during 1976. In April, a bus was involved in a tragic crash. Two men died and a third was injured when the car they were driving was in collision with a bus at the junction of Oliver's Brae and Seaforth Road, considered to be an accident blackspot. The driver of the bus, which was not carrying any passengers at the time, was uninjured. In June it was reported that vandals had 'indulged in an orgy of destruction' inside a bus which had been parked outside the garage in Bayhead Street. Every seat in the bus had been slashed with a knife, causing damage which was reckoned to cost at least £100 to repair. Ian Mitchell said, 'We have had instances of vandalism before, but nothing on this scale.'

In 1976 Margaret Macdonald from Tolsta Chaolais became Mitchell's first lady driver. She had previously driven buses in Glasgow, and the Stornoway Gazette considered that she would find driving on the Stornoway town routes to be a 'simple task compared with the busy Glasgow routes.'

A lady at the wheel

Later the same year, the Stornoway Gazette announced the arrival of the first 'lady at the wheel.' The paper of 23 October reported that 'passengers using one of Mitchell's buses on the town routes this week were surprised to find that the five and a half ton 43-seater vehicle was driven by an attractive red-haired lady.' She was thought to be 'the first female PSV [Public Service Vehicle] licence-holder in Lewis.' To allay any passengers' concerns it was added that she had been driving for eight years, the last four of which had been for Glasgow Corporation, with whom she had gained experience 'in all areas of Glasgow.' The reporter commented that the driver 'is employed on the town routes, which she no doubt finds a simple task compared with the busy Glasgow routes.'

17. MEMORIES: 'TOM' MACIVER

An interview and a first job

I had left The Nicolson Institute in July 1966. It was one of the happiest days of my life. I had left my name with the local Labour Exchange, as the Job Centres were then called. In the form I completed I had specified my interest in cars and that a job in one of the local garages would be my preference. From the moment I completed that form I dreamt of the future when I would be one of the island's great mechanics.

On a very significant day in my life a very important message awaited me: I was to report to the boss in Mitchell's Garage, a Mr Ian Mitchell, the very next day, for an interview regarding a job as a petrol pump attendant. I was over the moon. As far as I was concerned, the job was mine. I had a very vivid imagination and had visions of 'stravaiging' around Stornoway in my own Bedford CA van, as mechanics from the garages would do, driving around the streets with the sliding doors wide open, smoking roll ups and whistling at the girls.

Once I came down from cloud ninety I began to think about the interview. Sleep did not come easy that night. I was too busy in my CA van. Next morning after my mother had 'splogged' me up in my best clothes and given me all the best of advice – 'Fiach gum bith thu snog,' 'Bheir leat hankie,' 'Na bitheadh do lamhan na do phòcaidean,' (Try and be nice, take your hankie, don't put your hands in your pockets) and so on – I set off.

Upon alighting from the bus and entering the garage I was ushered into Ian Mitchell's office. The interview itself was quite orthodox to begin with. The usual questions were asked. Who was I? Where did my father work? Why did I want to become a mechanic? And so on. In the middle of this interrogation a man in a brown dust coat entered the office and spoke to Mr Mitchell as if he (the man in the brown coat) was the boss. 'Here,' he said, 'don't you remember that you're supposed to do the bus run to the airport today?'

'Oh hell!' said Mr Mitchell, 'you're right.' Mr Mitchell turned to me and said, 'Here cove, when can you get the next bus home?' I told him I could get the ten past one bus to Tolsta. Before I could say cove, I found myself travelling at great speed in a forty-two seater Bedford bus heading for Stornoway Airport. During this hectic journey it was explained to me that the man in the brown dust coat was none other than the legendary Kenny 'Keose'. I could never have believed then how much laughter this wonderful character was to bring to my life. The rest of my interview took place as I helped Mr Mitchell hump a very large load of heavy boxes from the cargo room of the airport on to the bus, and then unload them again at the bus station in Stornoway. We then drove back out to Bayhead Street and parked outside the garage. 'You can start on Monday, cove,' said Mr Mitchell. I WAS IN!

'How much are they going to pay you?' asked my mother. I did not know. I did not ask. I did not care. The first thing I needed to do was to get myself the regulation mechanics clothing. Denim jacket, denim jeans and black boots. I was now ready to begin my career in the Motor Trade.

On Monday morning I arrived for work along with everyone else at nine o'clock. My training for the job as petrol pump attendant took approximately half an hour in the company of a big lad from Sheshader in Point called Ivor Maclean, who, because of my arrival, was to be promoted to apprentice mechanic. I could tell he was anxious to get on with his new job and this was the reason for the brevity of my training. There were three pumps. One dispensed Regular petrol, one Super petrol, and the third Diesel. They were fairly simple to operate. The Regular cost four shillings and five pence per gallon and the Super and Derv cost four and nine per gallon. The rest of the training went as follows. 'You can check the engine oil level by pulling out the dipstick, wiping it with a rag (not supplied) sticking it back in again and observing the mark of the oil on the stick. The water goes in the radiator. Make sure you put it in the proper hole. The air-line is in the corner of the garage and it is free. It is about the only thing around here that is. The money the customer hands over is then given to the girl in the office. Cheerio and good luck to you. I'm off!' He vanished into the mysterious gloom of the garage entrance and I didn't see him any more that day.

There was a lovely girl in the office called Joan Mackenzie. She was a beauty queen. All the girls who worked in the office were very attractive, but there was not much I could do about that. I was too shy even to spend time in the office talking to them. I would stand outside, rain, hail or shine, while the other older boys chatted them up. I was quite happy just to be part of the empire that was Mitchell's. I worked

Left: Driving lessons were offered in the late 1960s and 70s.
Top right: The bus bay at the back of the garage on Matheson Road.
Iain 'an Tony and Dan Ferguson attend to some repair work.
Bottom right: The Parts Department.
Overleaf: At the 'hatch.' Dolly Green from Tolsta and Ian Mitchell
are served by 'Dodo' from Tolsta and Angus Macdonald.

a five day week. Mondays, Wednesdays and Saturdays my hours were 9am until 9pm. Tuesday was my day off, and Thursdays and Fridays I worked 9am till 6pm. My take home pay for this week was three pounds and one shilling (£3.05). The amazing thing was that I took home quite a lot of money in tips. The fuel was so cheap that if I did check someone's engine oil or tyre pressures they would more often than not give me a few pennies.

The stance that old Bodach (old man) Mitchell had acquired for his garage was ideal. It was the perfect place to capture the traffic coming in and out of Stornoway, particularly for fuel sales. Consequently I did not have much time within the working day for myself. My father had told me before I started work, never to be idle. 'If you find yourself with time on your hands, pick up a brush and sweep the floor,' he said. 'Do not stand around doing nothing.' He need not have worried, there was not much time for that. One of my duties each morning was to 'dip the tanks'. This meant I had to check how much bulk fuel we had in storage in the underground tanks situated in front of the garage. All this meant was that I had to insert a long dipstick into the tank and record a reading, then order the fuel as required. It was then delivered by road tanker from the BP depot on Shell Street. It always mystified me that the fuel for the Esso, BP and Shell petrol stations came out of the same tank, yet were sold as different products. I did not realise it at the time, but being at these petrol pumps all day and meeting so many people was taking me out of my shell. I began to get to know some of the regulars quite well.

I did six months on the pumps. I then went into the garage. I was mending punctures and washing cars. Ian came and told me that Angus Macdonald in the Parts Department was going on holiday and would I come and give a hand there. I turned up in the Parts Department on the following Monday and Ian took me through the process of identifying the different bits and pieces, and answering the phone. I was very shy at the time. Ian stayed with me for three days and then he went off to Glasgow for a Vauxhall meeting, and left me to it, so I was dropped in it, but it was a good way to learn it. When Angus came back, I joined him, and I was there for fifteen years. In the Parts Department everything had to be recorded – eventually Angus left and I got the parts manager's job, and got my own office and a company car.

Characters in the 1960s

Kenny 'Keose', Kenny Macaulay from Keose, was the transport manager at the time; he was in charge of the buses, the organising of the drivers and shifts. The maintenance of them was done by various guys, it just depended who was available. All the mechanics were quite qualified to repair anything, they had to be, whether it was a commercial vehicle, a car or whatever. In the office you had the girl who did the car insurance, there was also car hire, there was a lady there called Ina Matheson who was there for most of her life, there was Ishbel from Ness, there was Chrissie from Westview Terrace, Chrissie Macdonald who came in to do the insurance, so it was a massive complex really in the 60s.

The Parts Department was run by a guy called Angus Macdonald from Shader, Barvas, and when I went into the Parts Department he was my supervisor. There were three people in the Parts Department when I started; there was Angus and there was a lady who used to come in and do the stock control.

Now if I remember rightly Kenny 'Keose' took over from 'Jimsie' Afrin and later on the administrative side of things became a wee bit more complex so in order to allow the foreman to concentrate physically on what was going on in the workshop they brought on a lady, a sort of service department receptionist, who dealt with the job cards, did the paperwork and the filing; the paperwork was becoming a big thing.

The first one that I remember was Margaret Smith, who hails from Borve, married to a Glaswegian called Sammy, she was the first one and she was there for a number of years.

The bus station – there was a guy in there called Sergeant Davey Fraser, a big, big man, an ex-cop, he ran the show down there and his word was the law, he was one of the old style cops. You could go in there with parcels, or put them on the bus, or anything to do with the buses really, it was run from there.

The legendary 'Jimsie' Afrin

The foreman in the garage was a guy called 'Jimsie' Afrin; he was a bit of a legend. He was a pal of John, and had been there a long time. Inside the garage as you walked in was the foreman's office and there was a hand-painted sign on the door of the foreman's office saying, 'If you want a job done, ask for Jimsie.' The sign was in white writing on a blue wooden door.

When I started 'Jimsie' was off sick, and everybody was looking for this guy, people coming in saying, 'Where's "Jimsie"? Where's "Jimsie"?'

'Oh, he's off sick.'

'So who's in charge?'

It was Kenny 'Keose' who was running the garage then and it was this 'Jimsie' guy, everybody was looking for this 'Jimsie'. I had built up this image of 'Jimsie' Afrin as a tall, dashing handsome, swash-buckling guy, because I had never met him and one day this wee guy appeared wearing a tweed suit. This was the legend that was 'Jimsie' Afrin, not at all what I expected, but I spent many happy years with him until he retired. 'Jimsie' Afrin had been off work with a skin complaint which prevented him from working on any tools any more so he was promoted to car sales. So he then got the collar and tie on and the suit and he was put into the show room.

The Garage had a thing called a 'Black Hawk' engine diagnostic machine, which was bought at considerable cost then. It had dials and clocks on it and you hooked it up to a car and it was supposed to tell you the problem, but it wasn't an exact science. I remember one incidence where there was a car with a misfire and they had a problem diagnosing it, and they had actually tried the equipment belonging to one or two other garages on this vehicle – it was a Vauxhall – to try and diagnose it, and nobody could put it down. It was 'Jimsie' Afrin, who had then moved into the showroom, he came out one day and he told them to run the engine for him and he just listened to it and he said, 'If I were you I would remove the inlets, that's like an air thing, remove the inlet manifold and check it out.' Everybody thought, 'No, it can't be that, it can't be anything to do with that.' But they were that stuck that they tried it and sure enough there was a flaw – the inlet manifolds were like alloy – there was a flaw in the alloy and it had perforated it and allowed it to draw air which was causing it to misfire. So all the tools had failed but the man who listened to it solved the problem. That's the way these old guys worked, they depended solely on their own skill and talent to diagnose and do the job and they repaired things as opposed to just replacing them because Woody's (the local carrier) wasn't going to appear with it the next day.

Memories of Ian Mitchell

He was very fair, but to be a businessman he also had to drive a hard bargain. He could be pretty narky and crabbit and unsociable as an employer as well. He was there constantly when I started – he would be there in the morning when I would come in and he would be there when the last bus came in at night.

He took the reins when his father died and I think a lot of his father's generation turned against him because his philosophy was that someone he knew would come in for a battery on Tuesday and he would say I will pay for it on Friday and the bodach would say that's fine but when Ian did his training if you wanted a battery on Tuesday you paid for it on Tuesday. And that was his philosophy and I think a lot of people turned against him for that but that was the way to run the business.

There was always winding people up, all the usual pranks. When Angus arrived we had great fun, Angus was one of these guys always up to something, nothing bad, if he saw an opportunity to skive. I remember one day he went down town at lunchtime and he got a bucket of fresh mackerel on the quay and it was that time of year what you call *an fhuthar* in Gaelic or the 'dog days', the end of July beginning of August when you don't leave fish lying about because it will go off. So he had this pile of mackerel and he said I'm going to gut these here, so he went into the wee toilet in the stores and he said, 'I'm going in here with them and if anyone is looking for me I'm in the toilet.' So he's in this toilet with a wee knife and the bucket gutting the mackerel. Who came round looking for him but Ian Mitchell. 'Where's Angus?' I said, 'he's in the toilet. Can you come back?'

'Oh no, I'll wait' he says. So he came into the Parts Department and he was talking to me there. He was looking at his watch and Angus wasn't coming. In the end he went to the toilet door and he started 'Are you in there cove?'

Angus replied, 'Yes, Ian.'

'What are you doing?'

'What do you think I'm doing?'

So eventually Angus had to give up and open the toilet door and appear with a knife in his hand and blood on his wrists – caught in the act.

In the Parts Department Lucas had a scheme called the B90 scheme – when you bought a starter or a dynamo you returned the old one and it was sent away for reconditioning – it was an exchange scheme. So we used to send a van out every Tuesday to collect the old units from the garages in Stornoway and Angus was the man. He had this van all decalled out with the Mitchell's blue and yellow logo and Lucas badges – very conspicuous and caught the eye, and he was wearing a blue dustcoat with a badge on it and he saw an opportunity to skive so he was on Cromwell Street with the van parked at Maciver and Darts shop and he was getting some shopping and he met this guy from Borve with a collie dog on a lead and the guy knew him and he said,

Overleaf: Behind the 'hatch' – a view of the well-organised Parts Department.

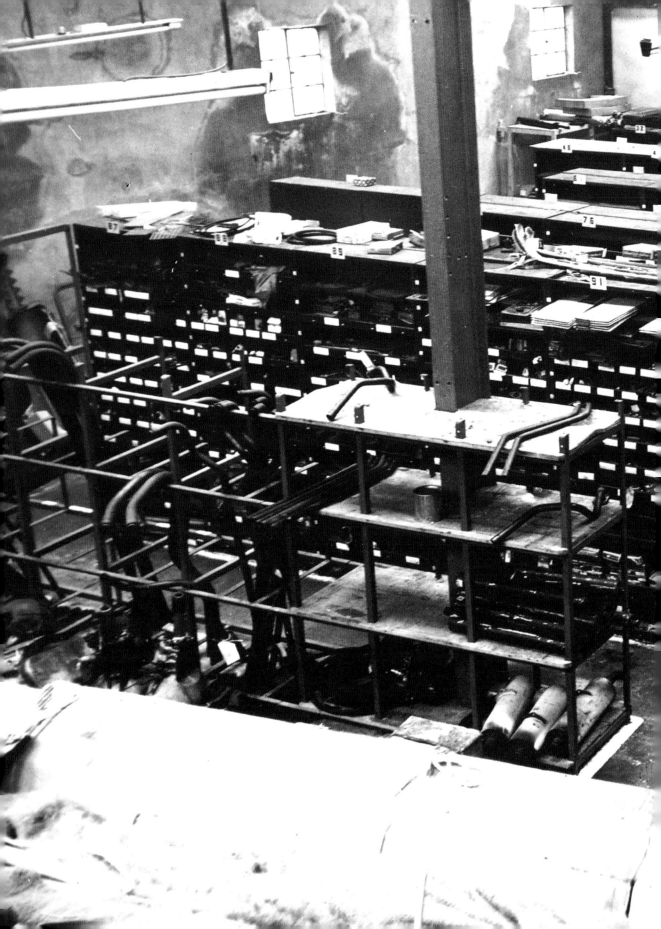

'I've got to go into Woolworths for a message, I can't take this dog in, can you hold the dog for me until I come back, I'll not be five minutes,' so Angus said, 'Yes, go for it', and he's standing there on Cromwell Street with a dog on a rope with his van and his coat, and who passes but Ian Mitchell driving 1 BUS. Ian stopped and asked, 'Hey cove, are we selling dogs now?'

A lorry came to the pumps from the mainland and it was a company called SPD and it was a new driver and it was a new girl started at the pumps. He told her to fill it up so she filled it up with petrol by mistake – she didn't know – and the guy had to catch the ferry in an hour's time. We were all going to lunch, but one of the guys agreed to stay during lunch break and that he would drain the tank so they put the lorry on one of the bus pits, drained all the petrol into an old metal dustbin, pushed the lorry out, filled it with diesel and off the guy went on the ferry. So we have three dustbins full of petrol in this pit and then the mechanic went off to his lunch. We came back from lunch and the boy who was working on the buses drove a bus on to the pit, went down the pit with his hand lamp, the bulb cracked against an iron beam, two bins went up in flames. The bus had not been immobilised and they managed to get it reversed off. We then didn't have fire extinguishers; we had put the fire out with a tarpaulin by the time the fire engine came. There was always something going on, it was hard work but fun all the time – the conditions dictated that you had to have some kind of levity or fun in amongst it.

Ian was a very kind man. He came to me one day – I used to work Christmas Day stocktaking within the Parts Department – he allowed me time off to attend amateur dramatics on the mainland. He came to me and said, 'what else do you do in your spare time?' – I said I'd just taken up fresh water fishing . A few days later he said, 'how are you getting on with the fishing?' I said, 'Oh all right but I need to get some gear.' He says, 'what do you need?' 'I need quite a lot, really.'

'All right', he says, 'lets go.' We jumped in the car, we went down to Meg's shop and we walked in and Ian asked me what do you need. I said, 'everything – a reel and a rod.' So I got my reel and my rod my hooks, my floats, my line, everything I need, free gratis and for nothing off him – that was the kind of man he was. We worked evenings if there was a project on – we never got overtime, I never asked for it, I never expected it.

Garage conditions in the 60s

The conditions were very poor – this was before the renovations took place. The Parts Department was always fairly good but in the garage there were no hoists or things like that – the boys worked in the pits which meant that they were up to their ankles in water a lot of the time because the water was coming in underground so it was then pretty primitive. The Health and Safety regulations were got by in other ways. It was cold, wet, damp – there was nothing but steel beams, concrete and corrugated iron, there was no heating. I remember we joined the union eventually and we went on strike for better conditions.

There was Ian's office and a common office and the accountant girl's office through the back. There was Eagle Star Insurance and there was a driving school at one time – Davie Macfarlane was the driving instructor. That was phased out in the mid-1960s.

On the Matheson Road side was the body shop – about seven or eight men were employed there – there was another seven or eight in the mechanics side, and there were two or three employed to maintain the buses. In 1966 it was a big business, as there were all the buses as well. It had been down-sized then as previously there were the quarries in Uig, and the lorries hauling sand as well.

It was a busy petrol station because there were few other pumps; this was the main one because it was drive-through.

I worked in the Parts Department and I would get a phone call from somebody in Ness or Harris and 'Can you put it on the bus for me?' and we did that and trusted them and they paid the driver.

There was a story of the guy that came with the demo machine for flooring – the garage floors were then greased up, they were thick with grease. This guy came along from the mainland with a kind of scarifier and he took the grease off down to the concrete. Old Mitchell asked him for a demonstration of it and he allowed him to do about half the garage and then he decided he didn't want it but he'd had his garage cleaned because there was about an inch of grease on the floor.

18. MEMORIES: ANGUS MACDONALD

I started work at Mitchell's in 1960 and I moved away to the mainland to work in 1972. When I came home from the army there were various jobs, but I tried Mitchell's. I had been a clerk in the Army, involved in logistics, ordering materials for tanks, and lorries. I got a start in the Parts Department, having had an interview with Mitchell himself and Ian as well. £9 a week was the going rate at Mitchell's – we used to get the bus home for nothing when we finished at six o'clock.

In the Parts Department were batteries and all the parts – it was mostly Vauxhall that we were catering for – Vauxhall motors and the Bedford vans and lorries. We did have the Fiat agency and we had the Standard vans. The first Fiats that came to the island came to Mitchells, he got the franchise, and it was the wee Fiat 500. We kept spare parts for Vauxhall, Bedford, Fiat, Standard and we also had the Lucas agency for all the electrical stuff – dynamos, starters, alternators, lighting, everything electrical that was in the cars.

We ran a stock control system. We got all the parts from the mainland – SMT Glasgow was the main Vauxhall Bedford supplier at that time. There were no computers like today, but a card index system – we ran a monthly stock order system, you ordered to keep a three month supply, bringing the balance up to the monthly stock, for example if you stocked ten and sold four you would order six to maintain the stock. If it was a busy item you carried a stock of about twenty. The goods used to come on vans, and Lucas themselves would come across with a lot of stock. Most of the exhaust systems, silencers and clamps, came by van, sometimes delivered by Pentland Auto Supplies in Inverness. If it was a specialist part it would be specially ordered and would come in about two days. As soon as the parts came in whoever had ordered it received a postcard to come and get it fitted, or sometimes they took it away and fitted it themselves. These were parts both for the public and for the mechanics in the garage. A stock was also carried especially for the buses, knowing that they would be used, especially the springs and hangers, for underneath, all the heavy stuff. If buses went off the road for some reason the parts would be there, the buses had to be kept on the road. Sometimes there would be a new problem on a bus, so two parts would be ordered as it was highly likely that another one would be required once they started wearing away.

It was a good system. There were two lasses as well – one was running the card index system keeping the stock control. She was working in the same area of the garage. The other was looking after the cars in the showroom, giving them a polish up, then tidying up in the parts. The main girl in the office was Ina Matheson – she was there for years and years. The overall boss of the office was called Isabel from Ness. Ina Matheson was running the accounts department.

John Mitchell was abrupt at times but he was respected; he knew he had a good squad working for him and he respected them, and the squad working in the garage were good mechanics, and they respected him. If you weren't good he would tell you, he was straight. John could pick the good ones out, within a week you would know if you were going to stay there for a long time or not. Other times he would see someone going into the office and he would say, 'Oh well, I think you should stop on Friday, and the guy would know why. So he had the best mechanics on the island, and they were the old-style mechanics, these boys repaired, they would get anything going.

John Mitchell was a good man. When my father and two men from Ness were coming home during the war on leave on the 'Lochness' and everything was black with the blackout conditions, they came off the 'Lochness' expecting to have walk across the Barvas Moor to walk home as there were no buses. They came past Mitchell's Garage, everything was pitch black, and they saw a light in Mitchell's office so they stopped and popped in, thinking somebody might have a car to run them home. It was Mitchell himself that was there and they asked him if there was any chance of someone running them over to Ness and Shader. He said, 'yes, I'll run you over.' He took them over to Ness. They went to pay him and he said, 'No, I don't want a penny. You boys are coming home on leave, maybe we'll never meet again, with the war, and I wish you all the best. I don't want a penny off you. Just enjoy your week's leave at home.'

He could be an awkward man at times, but he was good.

Ian said he wasn't made for the garage business but he carried it on very well, he was straightforward, a good laugh at times, was never seen to be angry; he would give you a hint now and again, but he was too kind-hearted; that's why we stood by him all the time, we appreciated the way he was. He would give you a blast now and then, just to show you he was the boss.

He had this uncanny way of always popping up when you didn't expect it. There was one instance when we heard he was going away for a couple of days to Glasgow on the plane. A lot of the boys had their own cars and as soon as he left the cars were brought into the garage, they were jacked up on axle stands, and the boys were working on a bearing or the back wheel, or the steering or whatever. Then someone announced, 'He's back!' Ian walked in: 'Hey cove, what's going on here?' What had happened was that the plane was late, delayed by two hours, and the boys in the garage didn't know. Ian had decided rather than stay at the airport he would come back to the garage. He gave the boys a blast, but didn't really mind.

There was a service called the P90 service, which was dynamos, alternators, starter motors, fuel pumps replaced old for new. I would go round the island garages and end up with the van packed with dynamos, starters and so on. They would be sent away in return for new stock. I had a white coat with Lucas P90 written on it. This day I was in town, and when I was coming round the corner where Maciver and Dart's was. This guy I knew was standing there and he had a sheepdog with him. He waved to me to pull in, so I did. He said, 'Can you hold the dog for me, I've got to dash for a message.' So I was standing on the pavement, holding the dog. Ian Mitchell pulled in with the Velox, DJS 98, pulled down the window and said, 'hey cove, are we selling dogs on the P90 exchange now?' I didn't know what to say, and started blubbering something and Ian said, 'Never mind, get on with your work.'

John Mitchell knew what to do and what to say at the right time. He was a clever businessman. I remember when NATO was coming to the airport and they had to extend the runways. This crowd were back and fore wanting to get the right kind of grit stone that would take the weight of the heavy planes. They were coming to Mitchell's for a taxi. They were all over the island and they found the proper grit in a quarry in Uig. Mitchell took them over to the quarry in a taxi and during the journey they must have been talking or John heard them on a phone describing how the stone was perfect for the airport. Mitchell dropped them off, and before they were back in Glasgow Mitchell had bought the quarry. No-one knew anything about it until one day about six tipper lorries arrived at the garage; Mitchell had bought the lorries and every ton of stone that went to the airport was carried in Mitchells lorries or others that he had contracted. That's how shrewd he was. He would seize any opportunity.

I remember the day when the coffins were going on the bus, before there was a hearse, going over to Lochs and Harris. They would have a coffin in the bus, with the people in the bus. One of the mechanics was a very nervous guy and he was once on a late run to Balallan and he had a coffin in the back of the bus. He was all right until all the passengers had got off and then he lost his nerve, and he said, 'Before I got back to town my hair was standing on end.'

John decided that we could have the hire of a small Bedford van on a Friday night, provided that we paid so much a mile. One guy would stay reasonably sober – he'd be the driver – and we'd take it to dances. Mitchell would read the speedo in the morning when we took the van back, and we used to pay him for the miles we'd done. Then one of the mechanics decided he would go under the van and disconnect the speedometer cable, and it didn't register anything then. We drove all over the place, and then we'd reconnect the cable when we were about two miles from town. This Saturday morning we told Mitchell, 'Oh, about twelve miles, we were in Laxdale and took a couple of boys to Point.' And Mitchell replied, 'No, you weren't, you were over in Leurbost and Balallan. I was talking to you over there.' Mitchell twigged on right away that we'd disconnected the speedo. We never got a van again. It didn't matter how kind he was, there was always somebody trying to do him.

THE MAY OUTING

Maclean, Chrissie B: The Stornoway I Knew,
Stornoway Historical Society, 2009

May Holiday was a very pleasant break from routine. Outings were planned and Mitchell's buses were booked by the various mills. Other groups like the YMCA, the Laxdale and the Stornoway Choirs and football teams all had buses booked for the day.

The favourite destinations were Tarbert, Uig, Ness, the Garry Sands and the Callanish Stones... The bus parties set out in high spirits with an accordionist, a piper and perhaps a keg of ale to liven the proceedings. The ladies would arrange the catering. There would be a bucket of salt herrings and potatoes. A big urn of tea and plenty of scones and sandwiches completed the picnic. Somewhere along the way they would stop and cook their meal on a peat fire...

When the destination was reached, be it Ness, Harris or Uig, the revellers set out to explore the surroundings or visit friends and relatives. In the evening, there were always concerts and "danns a' rathaid" in every village... As the buses streamed back into town in the late evening, the revellers were tired but happy and the day was the talking point for long afterwards.

19. NO MORE BUSES

As passenger numbers continued to decrease and running costs increased all the island's bus owners came to rely more and more on the subsidies provided by the Western Isles Council, thus increasing the Council's involvement with running the island's buses. In October 1979 a suggestion was made that the Council should take over the task of licensing bus routes and controlling fares from the Traffic Commissioners. Councillor Malcolm Macleod of Shawbost thought the system would be better served by a body which had local knowledge. He said the he 'had seen Commissioners with Ordnance Survey Maps going round the island to familiarise themselves with locations'. The Chief Executive, Roy Maciver, thought the Council would not know enough about the workings of the Traffic Commissioners. Control continued with the Commissioners.

By late 1979, however, there was dissatisfaction over the subsidies being offered. In November, several of the operators, now under the aegis of the Western Isles Bus Operators' Association, met in the offices of Mitchell's Garage to discuss the Council's offer. This included offers of a three-year subsidy agreement to pay the subsidies quarterly in arrears, depreciation on vehicles over an eight year period, ten percent on fares, and a more generous method of estimating depreciation. There was one clause in the offer which caused a major problem: this was that the Council should have the authority to specify fares, and the frequency and timing of the services. None of the operators accepted the deal. After the meeting Ian Mitchell said they would be seeking a further meeting with the Council as soon as possible, stating, 'The operators feel this (proposed agreement) would be giving control of their businesses to the Council, without the Council having any shares in these businesses'.

Ian Mitchell had a further cause for dissatisfaction, saying that no subsidies had been received from the Council for two years. The Council's response to this was that they had paid a subsidy for 1977 but not the following year as Mitchell's claim had been submitted late.

The other bus operators eventually accepted the new agreement. However, it would appear that Ian Mitchell and the Western Isles Council were unable to settle the matter amicably. Ian considered that the possibility of joint control between himself and the Council could not form a workable basis. He then felt he had no choice but to make the decision to cease running his services and to close down both his bus companies. Thus the dispute over 'who controls who' was to lead to the closure of the two bus companies operated by Ian Mitchell, John Mitchell (Stornoway) Ltd and Western Lewis Coaches Ltd, bringing to an end the bus operating companies started by his father sixty years earlier. The one bus operation John Mitchell started in 1921, which had developed into Mitchell's Transport & Parcels Service and then into one of the largest transport operators on the island, finally trading under the name John Mitchell (Stornoway) Ltd and under the control of his son Ian, was to come to an end.

The editor of the Stornoway Gazette, however, had a different opinion. In the leader article of 20 December 1979, he wrote 'it does seem that all avenues available to settle the matter amicably and without loss of jobs have not been fully explored.' The article went on to suggest that with the seriousness of the situation the possibility of appointing an independent arbiter could have been considered, and that the deadlock could then have been broken and a solution reached. Closing down the companies without a doubt put the Council on the spot. They had to act quickly to provide alternative transport for areas which were still dependent on public transport. It was also pointed out that to replace Mitchell's company might well cost more than to accede to his demands. Ian Mitchell, however, stated that it would 'take a miracle' to stop the impending closure. The Gazette editor hoped that 'even at this eleventh hour that miracle is still possible.'

On 22 December an announcement in the Gazette appeared regarding the services provided by John Mitchell (Stornoway) Ltd and Western Lewis Coaches Ltd. It simply stated 'All bus services operated by the above will cease on 31 December, 1979.' Ian Mitchell had decided to discontinue all their services rather than give total control of fares and services over to the Council. He stated 'the Council are taking over the bus operators' business via the back door – ie without buying any shareholding. We have offered the Council full consultation rights and even agreed not to make any changes without their approval in writing. This was also turned down.'

MITCHELL'S

AND

WESTERN LEWIS COACHES LTD

——

ALL BUS SERVICES OPERATED BY THE ABOVE WILL CEASE ON 31 DECEMBER, 1979

Top: A view of the bus station in 1973. Although it is busy with buses, passenger numbers were declining and services struggling to pay. Bottom: In December 1979 Ian decided to withdraw all the bus services run by the two companies as a result of a dispute with the Council over subsidies. The public discovered this information by means of this small advertisement placed in the Stornoway Gazette.

Most of Mitchell's drivers pictured as they changed shift for the last time.
From left to right are Calum Morrison, Murdo Macleod, Margaret Macdonald,
Murdo A Mackay, Daniel Macsween, Angus Maciver, Donald Maciver and Angus Maclean.

The impending result of this was that fifteen drivers, mechanics and clerical workers employed by the two bus companies would be made redundant. The drivers were unanimously behind their employer's decision, although concerned about their forthcoming employment prospects. One of the drivers said 'We're totally behind the company. The Council are trying to take us over without owning the buses.'

The Council's response to the situation was to seek alternative arrangements to provide services to the areas which would be affected. The Chief Executive stated that he expected the matter to be remitted to the Transport Committee, which would deal with it as a matter of urgency.

With the situation at this delicate stage, the next development was the sight, shortly after 1 pm on 19 December 1979, of five of Mitchell's buses in their blue livery arriving in front of the Council offices and being strategically placed to create a blockade, preventing any other traffic from leaving or entering. The drivers demanded a meeting with Council officials and were promised that the Chief Executive would see them within the hour. The Council's stance was put to the drivers by the Chief Executive, who said, 'We spoke to a number of Mr Mitchell's drivers who called at the office today and explained our position. I emphasised to them that the withdrawal of services by Mr Mitchell, whilst being regretted by the Council, was entirely a matter for the Traffic Commissioners.

Top: In protest at the situation, and possible redundancies, the drivers used five buses to blockade the Council offices, maintaining they would keep them there until either an agreement was reached or the police towed the buses away.
Bottom: The headline in the Stornoway Gazette stated 'The Buses are Back,' adding, '"What now?" seems to be the question posed by bus driver Murdo John Mackenzie as Mitchell's buses park at the bus station for the last time.' After Ian withdrew the services, other operators took over buses, the routes and the drivers.

'There was no question of the Council withdrawing subsidies from Ian Mitchell's bus services. The only point in question was that he was being asked to enter into an agreement which would mean payment of subsidies on a more generous basis in return for an obligation to implement changes in times and frequencies of journeys if requested to do so.'

There was clearly no leeway being offered by the Council, especially as the Chief Executive added that he did not consider the Council's position unreasonable.

The drivers had earlier stated that the buses would remain in front of the Council offices until either an agreement was reached or the police towed the buses away. Indeed, two police officers had arrived shortly before the drivers met with the Chief Executive. However, after the meeting, the TGWU shop steward announced that the vehicles were to be removed and the drivers were going to consult further with their management.

The day after the bus blockade a further meeting was held between Ian Mitchell and senior Council officials, but still they could not reach any agreement. Ian asked for payment of his subsidies for 1979, having finalised his accounts. He was told, however, that it was impossible to put this request before the Transportation Committee that day, and not before the Committee next met, which was not until 7 February 1980. It was suggested that if Ian required immediate cash assistance the Council could recommend payment of a sum suitable to enable him to continue operating his buses until the meeting in February. Ian Mitchell rejected these suggestions, saying that he still intended to cease his operations on the last day of the year. He continued to refuse to sign a three-year subsidy contract which would have given the two companies a subsidy of at least £26,000 a year, maintaining still that giving the council powers to change times, frequencies and routes of buses amounted to 'municipalisation of the business.' He also intended to dispose of his buses, saying, 'I will accept any reasonable offer for my buses.' On the last day of December 1979 the two bus companies thus ceased to trade.

It goes without saying that there were gloomy predictions that nine bus routes throughout the island would be without bus services from the start of 1980, but as things turned out they proved to be unfounded. Three operators were willing to take over the services, and the Western Isles Council stepped in quickly to ensure there was a continuation of all the routes, with services commencing in the first week of 1980. Applications were immediately submitted to the Traffic Commissioners who with the same rapidity granted road service licences. Lochs Motor Transport took over the Stornoway town routes and the West Side circular, Galson-Stornoway Motor Services were to run the service to Ness, while William Macdonald agreed to operate the run to Tolsta and Back, with almost all the routes maintaining the same schedules.

Ian Mitchell paid tribute to all who had been involved in the bus operations over the sixty years of its existence, saying, 'We were fortunate over the years in having a good staff, a good maintenance record, a good safety record and dependable drivers.' He clearly felt that it was a nostalgic time, but more prosaically, and modestly, considered that over the years their record had not been a bad one.

One of Mitchell's buses was taken over by Lochs Motor Transport and arrangements were made with the Stornoway Pier and Harbour Commission for the new operators to use the bus stance on Cromwell Street quay. This was previously let to Western Lewis Coaches Ltd, but the let was easily transferred. The building at the bus station was owned by Mitchell's, and the Pier and Harbour Commission had the option of purchasing the building from Ian Mitchell or asking him to demolish it. The Council also agreed at the time to continue the national Concessionary Fares Scheme which was operated by the bus companies.

It was, without a doubt, the end of an era in Stornoway and throughout the island. For years, the blue buses, almost all Bedfords, had been synonymous with travel into town from Ness, the West Side and Tolsta, and equally they were a familiar sight in Stornoway as they negotiated the junctions and parked vehicles as they served the outlying parts of town. This was the end of operating buses for Ian Mitchell, but it was not the end of the bus companies. Although no buses had been owned and no services operated, it was not until May 1990 that Western Lewis Coaches Ltd was finally dissolved and the name removed from the Register of Companies.

20. THE BUS FLEET

Mitchell's Transport & Parcel Service/ John Mitchell (Stornoway) Ltd

From his beginning in 1921, John Mitchell built up his fleet to become the largest in the island, reaching a maximum of thirty-eight vehicles in 1962. His first bus was probably a second-hand Garfield or Overland, and thought to be a converted ambulance, built by the Willys-Overland Motor Co in America for service in the First World War. It was able to carry sixteen passengers and, like many subsequent purchases, carried a Ross & Cromarty registration number, in this case JS 1040. This vehicle survived until 1926, the years of jolting and bumping on the poor road between Shawbost and Stornoway eventually taking its toll. This bus was followed by two more Overlands, purchased in 1922 and 1926. The first of these, supplied by 'Dondie' Maciver was recorded as a van but licensed as a hackney with one seat; the second vehicle was also a van, and had seats for passengers fitted.

During the 1930s John Mitchell purchased a variety of makes, some new but mostly second-hand. The makers were Ford, Gilford, Chevrolet, Dodge Albion and Commer. The first of many Bedford buses was obtained in 1932. It was another one supplied by John's uncle, 'Dondie' Maciver, and although recorded as being for goods only, this was probably the first bus to be operated by Mitchell's Transport and Parcels Service. By 1934 the company owned four coaches, two lorries and three vehicles for private hire. It was during the 1930s that John Mitchell started building bus bodies, and a number of his own vehicles were completed by him. There seems to have been no specific company livery at the time. Buses were recorded as being painted green and cream, maroon and cream, green, brown and even grey at various times. During the War no fewer than sixteen new (to Mitchell) buses were added to the fleet, with five being withdrawn.

Top left: A typical example of the utility buses which Mitchell's operated in the years just after World War Two. YJ 7856 was a Bedford OB with a body built by John Mitchell. Top right: Often to be seen on the Harris service in the 1950s and early 1960s was JS 9744, a Bedford with a Duple body. Middle left: The standard Mitchell bus of the 1960s was a Bedford SB with a Duple body, as seen in this typical view of the bus station. Middle right: JS 8350 was an SCWS bodied Austin dating from 1949 and is seen here outside the Rendezvous Café in Cromwell Street. This bus, which was owned by Western Lewis Coaches, would have been scrapped before the company was taken over by John Mitchell in 1960. Bottom left: John purchased a number of Bedford buses with Duple bodies such as this one, pictured at the bus station in Stornoway. Bottom right: A number of buses ended their days as an àirigh (sheiling) or shed on the moor.

Pictured here on North Beach Quay is this Bedford, EJS 408, which was owned between 1958 and 1965.

It was not until just after the Second World War, in 1946, that the first bus painted in what became the standard livery of blue and white first made an appearance when the Bedford JS 6702 appeared, although before that was finally adopted, the colour scheme used was dark blue with light blue round the windows.

Between 1946 and 1969, no fewer than fifty-two Bedford vehicles were to enter the fleet, again some being new, while others were purchased second-hand. Some of the buses remained on service for many years while others were only in the fleet for a short time. Most of the Bedfords were of two types. The majority of those purchased between 1943 and 1950 were the OB type. These were very familiar on the island, having a bull-nose front and had bodies built either by Duple or SMT. The cost of a new Bedford OB before the Second World War was £1,314.10s. From about 1950 the OB was replaced by the Bedford SB; this model became the standard 'Mitchell's bus' of the 1960s and 70s. It was designed with the driver's seat located at the front of the vehicle, beside the engine, known as 'forward control'. The bodies of these buses were built either by Duple or Willowbrook.

Two of the Bedfords, purchased in 1946 and 1947, were thought to have had bodies built by John Mitchell from SMT spares, probably indicative of post-war shortages. One vehicle which was in the Mitchell fleet for eleven years started life as a demonstrator for

The last two buses purchased by Ian, in 1979, were Bedford SB5s with 'army' style bodies built by Marshall. They were used to transport workers to and from the oil-related works at Arnish.

Vauxhall Motors Ltd. Described as a 'Bedford Mark VI experimental bus', it had a coach body built by Duple, a well-known coach builder, but was fitted with bus seats. It had been leant out to Lincolnshire Road Car Co Ltd, but on being returned to Vauxhall Motors after a year it was acquired in 1954 by John Mitchell.

John Mitchell (Stornoway) Ltd.

During the 1960s the size of the fleet was reduced considerably, as buses were either scrapped, sold or transferred to Western Lewis Coaches Ltd. Those which were sold went to a variety of destinations, some to companies on the mainland as far afield as Arran and South Wales, while others remained on the island, having been bought by other operators such as Galson-Stornoway Motor Services Ltd and Lochs Motor Transport Ltd. About 1970 the Nicolson Institute purchased a vehicle for their own use; later, having been used for spares and become derelict, it ended up being used as a shed. Another bus became what was described as an 'immobile house.' The bus which had been involved in the fatal crash had suffered sufficient damage to be declared a write off.

Another 'different' vehicle became part of the fleet for a short time, between June 1964 and December 1965. This was another Bedford with bodywork by Duple; it was a VAL model, which was designed

A common spelling mistake! DJS 222 was owned by Mitchell's between 1958 and 1965
– it is not known how long the name appeared wrongly spelt.

with two front steering axles instead of the usual one. It was probably
not retained in the fleet because of its length; it would certainly have
had trouble negotiating some of the corners and junctions on the
town service.

The last two buses to be bought by Ian Mitchell were a pair of Bedford
SB5s, which were purchased new in September 1979. They were built
with 40 seat Marshall Bodies, and were the first Army-type buses built
in Britain by Marshall. One of the buses was registered with John
Mitchell (Stornoway) Ltd, the other under Mitchell's sister company of
Western Lewis Coaches. When Mitchell's services ceased to operate
both were initially retained and used to transport workers to and from
the oil-related industrial area which had opened up at Arnish, just
outside Stornoway. They were purchased in November 1983 by D.H.M.
MacIver, trading as Hebridean Transport, Island Road, Stornoway.
One subsequently became a driving school vehicle, while the other
ended up in Orkney.

Western Lewis Coaches Ltd

When John Mitchell took over Western Lewis Coaches Ltd in 1960,
the cream and green colour scheme of its buses was replaced by dark
blue and cream, so that the two fleets were indistinguishable. When
the two companies were reorganised and Western Lewis Coaches
took over the running of the majority of the services, five buses were

Ian added this Bedford VAL to the fleet in 1964. It was larger than the other buses, with a seating capacity of 51, compared to the standard 42. The bus was unusual in having two front axles. Unfortunately it proved to be too large for Stornoway's narrow streets and sharp corners, and was sold after only 16 months at the end of 1965.

transferred to that fleet. Between 1972 and 1979 seven new Bedford SB buses, of which six had Willowbrook bodies, were added. All of these were in service up to the time the company ceased trading. The newest bus actually only ran for two months before the services were stopped. The disposal of the fleet was similar to that already described for the buses of John Mitchell (Stornoway) Ltd. A number of the buses were taken over by the companies which had agreed to operate the services. The fate of a number of buses has not been recorded. Three of the vehicles became, respectively, a shed, a store and a builders' site hut, and some others, in various staged of disintegration, can still be seen lying on crofts on the island.

REGISTRATION NUMBERS

With the increasing popularity of personalised number plates representing people's names, places and company names, it is interesting that both John and Ian Mitchell found fascination with registration numbers. From the earliest days new vehicles were registered locally and therefore carried the Ross and Cromarty letters JS, familiar to all who live on Lewis.

It was in 1956 that the first 'interesting' number appeared. This was DJS222, on one of the ubiquitous Bedford buses. Then in 1960, GJS777 appeared. This was followed by JJS333 and JJS444 in 1961, KJS555 and KJS666 in 1962. Similar numbers were available after the change in the registration system in the early 1960s and AJS111B duly appeared in 1964, followed in 1965 by BJS999C, and DJS600D and EJS222D in 1966. 1967 saw EJS700E, EJS800E and EJS900E enter the fleet of Western Lewis Coaches, followed by JJS100G in 1969. Two years later came LJS500J, then RJS300L in 1973, JJS111P in 1976, KJS444R and KJS555R in 1977, and finally PJS700T appeared in 1979.

Ian Mitchell's cars were no less distinctive, being well known in Stornoway, carrying the very appropriate number, 1 BUS.

Opposite top: Some of the distinctive registration numbers carried by Mitchell's buses, and Ian's own car plate, 1 BUS.
Opposite bottom: Ian Mitchell's distinctive number plate, 1 BUS.

21. EVIDENCE OF MORE SUCCESS

Ian continued to develop his links with Vauxhall and to continue to develop the operations of the garage. The success of the Vauxhall-Bedford dealership was shown in 1978 when Mitchell's were awarded the six-plaque Euroservice Guild Award. This was a dealership motivation programme launched by Vauxhall Motors. This was designed to encourage the highest possible levels of after-sales service, and was awarded after a comprehensive inspection of the business had been made. The garage was one of only two Scottish dealers to achieve the standard. The Regional Service Manager for Vauxhall Motors, presenting the award, praised the work of Mitchell's, saying 'that for the very few dealerships who achieve Guild status this must be the culmination of their efforts and perhaps their dreams.' Receiving the award, Ian Mitchell replied, 'the Guild Award confirms our belief that right here, beneath Stornoway's blue suburban skies, we have a team that is hard to beat.'

The high standards continued to be maintained, as the award was received every year well into the 1980s. At the award ceremony in 1981, Ian Mitchell paid tribute to his staff, saying, 'at the end of the day it is not only buildings and equipment, but people that make things happen.' The Stornoway Gazette added, 'as an ideal acknowledgement to mark their Diamond Jubilee of sixty years in business, this third top award proves Mitchell's philosophy is right.' In recognition of the hard work involved in achieving these awards four of Mitchell's supervisors were rewarded with a trip to the United States.

Top: General Motors awarded Mitchell's Garage their Master Dealer Award for exceptional operating standards in 1984. Gaining this prestigious award meant that Mitchell's was the only Scottish dealer holding all three of GM's awards, Parts and Accessories Guild, Euroservice Guild and Master Dealer. This picture shows the staff back at work the morning after a celebratory evening. Ian Mitchell, still sipping champagne, said, 'We have to do better still, but meantime everyone here is happy with their achievement.'
Back row, from left to right: Dolly Macleod, Murdo 'Toots' Macleod, Angus 'Floppy' Macleod, Neil 'Fallon' Macarthur, Ian Mitchell, Colin Jack, Kenny 'Keose' Macaulay, Norman Macleod and Kenny Nicolson. Front row: Cathy (surname unknown), Joan Macleod, Chrissie Macdonald, Mairi Macleod, Mary Nicolson and Ina Matheson.
Bottom: An interior view of the garage.

Top: Celebrating the Vauxhall Quality Dealer Award, 1980s. Back row, left to right: Ina Matheson, Alex Mair, Ian Bobbans, Murdo 'Toots' Macleod, Angus 'Floppy' Macleod, 'Tom' Maciver, Donald John Macleod, Kenny 'Keose' Macaulay, Kenny Nicolson, Margaret Sutherland, Angus Campbell, Norman Macleod and Angus Murdo Campbell.
In front are Dolina Macarthur, Arthur Boath, Ian Mitchell, Chrissie Macdonald and Ian Coomber (Vauxhall Motors).
Bottom: The expanded and modernised garage in the 1970s.

The New York trip, remembered by 'Tom' Maciver

We went to America in 1981 in January – the reason for the trip was that Lewis Offshore was booming, the town was booming, Ian had sold the buses, he had two buses running continually from Arnish, the garage was busy, the car sales were good and that's the kind of guy he was. All the employees got some kind of rewards for their efforts and the fact that the company was making a bit of money. Kenny 'Kcosc' and I and a guy called Kenneth Nicolson, we were heads of departments so we got a wee bit extra. But everybody got something.

America – New York – he asked me about it – I didn't have a passport or anything so I had to go through all the passport stuff and eventually agreed that I would go. The foreman refused to go – he got rewarded in some other way. So we took off on a Monday morning from Stornoway and we were in New York that night and we spent a week there. This was my first trip abroad. It was in January and it was the coldest winter they'd had for thirty-seven years. So we did all the sightseeing and coming back we came back on the Saturday so we were there nearly the full week. New York at that time was not as safe as it is now – when we checked into the hotel the first thing the guy said to us was, 'You're on vacation, where are you from?' 'Scotland.' 'Right,' he said, 'when you go out there you don't talk to anybody, you don't window shop, you don't look as if you are tourists you just go about your business and ignore everybody because there are people out there and if they spot that you are a tourist they'll rob you.' We arrived late at night and went straight to bed, and the first day we went out I remember walking up to the kerb to cross the road and I felt this figure coming up beside me and it was an American cop with a gun. We had a great week there, we saw all the sights.

Ian Mitchell's commitment to the success of his business can be seen by his attendance at seminars and courses, always involving travel away from the island. This commitment is exemplified by his attendance at the 167th Dealership Management Conference held between 5 and 29 October 1981 at the General Motors Institute at Flint, Michigan USA.

In 1984, General Motors, now the owners of Vauxhall-Bedford, introduced an even higher category of dealer award for operating standards, called 'Master Dealer'. Mitchell's became one of only three dealers in the United Kingdom to achieve this award, and they were the only Scottish dealer to hold three separate awards, Parts and Accessories Guild Award, Euroservices Guild and Master Dealer. A celebratory evening was held at which Ian Mitchell, between sips of champagne, said, 'we have to do better still, but meanwhile everyone here is understandably happy with their achievement.'

A Volvo agency was offered in 1988, but Ian Mitchell declined to take this. Perhaps he was looking towards the future and retirement, and did not wish to take on further responsibility. In the same way, in 1990, the year when the Parts Department was relocated, Ian Mitchell reduced the area used to display vehicles covered by his dealership by fifty per cent. At the same time Ian took the unusual step of removing the roof from the showroom – without a roof the area was exempt from Council Tax.

Driving for Royalty

As an example of the standing with which Mitchell's was held, Ian Mitchell was asked to provide transport for Royalty and other dignitaries when they visited the island in 1978. A letter to Ian Mitchell from Major Samuel Longbotham, Lord Lieutenant, written in May 1978, thanks Ian for his help and support given to the Lieutenancy during the Queen's Silver Jubilee Appeal events held the previous year. In particular, he was thanked for the provision of transport during the Carnival and Fireworks Festival.

The following year Ian Mitchell was asked to provide transport during the Royal visit on 14 August to the Airport. This involved providing three cars, one for the Prince of Wales, Princess Anne and Lord Granville, a second for Princess Alexandra and her son and daughter, and the third to convey Angus Ogilvie [husband of Princess Alexandra]. For this purpose Ian chose to take the first group himself in his Vauxhall Royale, the long-serving 'Jimsie' Afrin would drive the second group in a Vauxhall Cavalier, while Mrs Chris Macdonald would follow with a Cavalier sports hatch as the third car. A letter from Major Longbotham to Ian Mitchell describes both the preparations for the occasion and the 'interesting route' that was chosen:

MAJOR SAMUEL LONGBOTHAM

25 Lewis Street,
Stornoway,
Isle of Lewis

29th April, 1980.

Telephone :
STORNOWAY 2519

Dear Iain,

Please accept my warmest thanks for your help
during the visit of H.R.H. The Prince of Wales to Stornoway
on Monday and Wednesday of last week.

The placing of your private car at the disposal
of the Lieutenancy and H.R.H.——and taking the wheel—— was a
splendid gesture on your part, and I am very much indebted
to you for your assistance and support.

Yours sincerely,
S. Longbotham.

Iain Mitchell, Esq.,
Mitchell's Garage,
Bayhead, Stornoway.

Top: Ian had the honour of driving the Prince of Wales when he visited Stornoway in 1980.
Bottom: Prince Charles and Princess Diana visited the Western Isles in 1985 and Ian again was the 'Royal driver'.
The Stornoway Gazette reported that 'the Royal couple were opening the doors of the car before the chauffeur,
Mr Ian Mitchell, ...and a security man could leap out to hold them open.'

Top: This is a 1904 Vauxhall which was on display in the showroom in 1983. Ian would use any method to help sell cars. Bottom: Ian chats to Maurice Willment of Vauxhall Motors on the occasion of being awarded a G M Euroservice Quality Dealer Award in February 1986.

The Council are having a brief rehearsal of people's positions etc on the afternoon of Monday 13 August at 2pm for the Royal Visit on 14 August. I would suggest that you and your drivers, if they have time, might care to be present – so that at least you can see where they are to be positioned. You will of course be after the cars detailed for the main Royal procession. There will be one police car detailed to accompany you. I do not mind how the party proceeds, either with the police car in the lead or following (but do not lose him).

I can discuss the actual route with you on Monday afternoon and while it must be subject to police approval at the end of the day, I would suggest that you go straight out South Beach Street, Shell Street, Ferry Road, Bells Road, Caberfeidh Road, in between Kenneth Mackenzie's mill and the gut factory, onto Seaforth Road and out to the airport. My reason for taking such a 'terrible route' is that it is all pretty terrible that way and I bet they are very rarely taken to see any place with the lid off! If, however, you do not want to take your car down those pot-holes, I will quite understand.

In order to convey his important passengers, Ian Mitchell was issued with a piece of paper headed 'TO WHOM IT MAY CONCERN' and stating, 'This is to clear Iain Mitchell, 3 Matheson Road, Stornoway, as Driver Number 1 of Prince Charles and Party on 14 August 1979.' Clearly security was more lax in those days!

In 1980, Ian Mitchell was again driving the Prince of Wales on the island. He was thanked for placing his own car at 'the disposal of the Lieutenancy and H.R.H.' and for 'taking the wheel,' all considered by Major Longbotham to be a 'splendid gesture on your part.'

Overleaf: Ian is congratulated by members of the Vauxhall Motors management team having completed a three-year dealership training scheme in June 1954.

EXTRACTS FROM THE
EMPLOYEES HANDBOOK 1977

We believe that every employee should have a period of rest and relaxation every year. Holidays with pay is one of the ways we show our appreciation to you for your length of service and good work.

As a personal incentive, any employee who introduced a NEW customer to the dealership, and as a result of this introduction buys a new or used vehicle from us, will receive an introductory commission of £10.

Some helpful tips to remember in dealing with our customers:

1 Greet customers promptly and courteously.
2 Smile.
3 Call customers by name (Mr, Mrs or Miss).
4 Be frank and honest.
5 Be friendly but not too familiar.
6 Don't argue or lose your temper.
7 Keep promises.
8 Show your appreciation. Say "Thank You."
9 Look the part.
10 Be tactful.

Our record of good citizenship is important to us. It is your responsibility to build good friendships for our company. Take as active a part in civic affairs as circumstances will permit, participate in charity and welfare drives, and exercise your right to vote in all elections, regardless of how unimportant they may seem.

Telephone practice

Telephones should be answered promptly. In order to determine the name of the calling party, use the phrase "Can I ask who is calling?" or similar. Do not say "Who is calling?"

Smoking when customers are present

All employees should refrain from smoking in the presence of our customers. When you are waiting on a customer, you are involved in serious business, and the relaxation or priviledge (sic) of smoking should not be going on at the same time. Let's show complete attention and respect for our customers by refraining from smoking in their presence.

Public Relations

The following are essential requirements:-

A personal appearance that is neat and clean and reflects a professional image.

A sympathetic understanding of customer attitudes and needs.

A pleasant and acceptable manner.

Remember – people buy from people they like, in places they feel their custom is welcome.

Rumours

Rumours have the habit of flying around from time to time, and some people delight in passing them on as the truth. When you hear a rumour, ask your supervisor if there is any truth to it. If he doesn't know, he can find out for you.

Company Rules (a selection)

You must not remove or take away any property belonging to the company or any other employee, as that is theft.

You must not fight, threat, intimidate or coerce fellow employees for any purpose.

You must not report for work under the influence of drink or drugs, or consume any alcoholic beverage on the premises.

You must not use obscene or abusive language, or spread malicious gossip or rumour.

Visitations to employees while at work, by their friends, should be held to a minimum and be of short duration, because this can interfere with the attention we give to our customers.

When an employee is more than 5 minutes late on 4 separate occasions within a 4 week period, this is deemed to be not acceptable and an appropriate warning given in accordance with the disciplinary procedure will be given.

Employees must not take away, or drive outwith the premises, any motor vehicle, whether the property of the company, or left in our care, except when approved in advance by their supervisor.

Horseplay and throwing things

Horseplay may be intended to be harmless, but can result in serious injury. Remember, your idea of a practical joke may cripple someone for life. It is also an offence under the Health and Safety at Work Act.

22. MEMORIES: RUAIRIDH MURRAY

I worked at Mitchell's from 1974 to 1979. I started as an apprentice mechanic, straight from school. Ian Mitchell would take on two apprentices every year – one went on to the buses, I went on to the cars. The first job I ever did for Ian Mitchell, I walked into the building and there he was, I had this toolbox with probably half a dozen wee spanners in it and he told me to put that over to the side there and to go and give another apprentice a hand. This was to take a battery over to Charlie Barley's [butcher's shop nearby] where Ian Mitchell would park the old O model Bedford breakdown wagon that he had. I was then to put the battery into it to start it – we were going out to do a job somewhere. This was my introduction to the garage.

Ian Mitchell was not hands on – never, no. He was very much a collar and tie man. He would be in the office and regularly you would see him, hear his footsteps, he had a very distinctive march – the shoes had tacks on the bottom of them, you could hear the man approaching, so you stopped the nonsense very quickly. There was quite a lot of apprentices so we would usually get a bit of boisterous behaviour, but certainly not when Ian came in.

When Ian was away things were very different in the garage. Not that the work wasn't done, it was; but Ian's wife, Anne, would come in just to see that everything was OK; she was fantastic, like chalk and cheese, she was such a lovely woman. Ian was as well, he was a really nice man. You had to be very, very careful, he would fly off the handle, he was quite temperamental, but he was the boss, he was paying out wages every week and if there was nonsense going on, God help you. Timekeeping was also an absolute must, you couldn't walk in there at five past nine.

I believe that to begin with there were no records kept. Ian had told me that he had got a row from the authorities for his record keeping – it was bits of paper, he would write it on a bit of paper, and when he was done it was put in a drawer. So he knew where everything was, but obviously that wasn't good enough for the authorities, so he got a couple of old books and started writing in them, just to get it a wee bit better. From then on books with every car, bus or lorry that Ian Mitchell bought and sold, whether it was taken in as a trade in or new, were all recorded, from 1965 to the last day.

The old garage was still standing but he was going to make it smaller so he built part of the new garage inside the old one. He had a big six wheeler Mack lorry, ex American Army, it was a 1939 and he used that to pull the walls away from the new garage – you wouldn't get away with that today, but that's what he did. The garage was in three stages – the big old building that was from Leverburgh, there was the bus garage from Back and then a third bit was just added on to it, making three distinct parts.

The roof was taken off because of the rates. He was telling me what he was paying in rates; this was the old showroom and stores and beside that was the bus park where there was a pit, that's where we worked; beside that was a wall, that was into the store, and forward into the car showroom, always a few brand new cars in there; and by taking the roof off that I think he put it down to something like a quarter of what he was paying. But he left the walls standing.

Tales of the breakdown trucks

One was an American Mack, and it was in England as a motorway recovery vehicle. It weighed about fourteen tons. Ian Mitchell and a guy called 'Dondie' Macdonald travelled down to drive it back up here. When it arrived here it was white with red writing on it. On the front was written 'The White Banshee'. It was painted with Mitchell blue and all the writing. It arrived around the seventies.

The second breakdown truck was the O model; it was a 1940s vehicle, and had belonged to Mitchell's from before the 1960s. It was a converted lorry, the back part with crane having been added. The van was a Bedford CA van with a Perkins engine. There was another vehicle, an Austin K9.

One Monday when the staff came in to work, they discovered that over the weekend the four vehicles had been titled, signwritten on the front, on the theme of Goldilocks and the three bears. There was Mammy Bear, Daddy Bear, Baby Bear, and the Austin was Snowy Bear.

REGISTRATIONS NUMBERS USED
STARTING FROM 1ST JANUARY 1965 →

BY
MITCHELL'S
BAY HEAD ST.
STORNOWAY
TEL
2888.

1 SATURDAY
New Year's Day

R 9·07 ☀ S 5·02

WEEK 1 · 1-365

WEEK 1 · 2 · 364

SUNDAY 2

BJS 560 C	8 cwt Van NAVY BLUE	D. J. MACRAY 8 LINSHADER UIG
BJS 579 C	FIAT 850 Saloon WHITE	Donald Campbell 101 Spey Rd. DARSDEN
BJS 580 C	FIAT 1500 L Saloon MAROON	D. H. M. McIVER 2 FERRY Rd SY
BJS 581 C	VICTOR ESTATE CAR.	MACLEAN BROS KEITH ST SY
BJS 582 C	Super VICTOR 101 SALOON BLACK	J. MACLEOD STOCKINISH HARRIS

NOTES

BJS 634 C	VOLKS. JAVA GREEN.	Dr. M. MACIVER LIVERBOST.
BJS 637 C	WORK BUS B.R. GREEN.	M MACDONALD 120 CROSS SKIGERSTA NESS
BJS 638 C	6 cwt VAN NAVY BLUE	J MACKENZIE 15 UPPER BAYBLE SY.

DECEMBER 1971	JANUARY 1972	FEBRUARY 1972	MARCH 1972
S 5 12 19 26	S 2 9 16 23 30	S 6 13 20 27	S 5 12 19 26
M 6 13 20 27	M 3 10 17 24 31	M 7 14 21 28	M 6 13 20 27
T 7 14 21 28	T 4 11 18 25	T 1 8 15 22 29	T 7 14 21 28
W 1 8 15 22 29	W 5 12 19 26	W 2 9 16 23	W 1 8 15 22 29
T 2 9 16 23 30	T 6 13 20 27	T 3 10 17 24	T 2 9 16 23 30
F 3 10 17 24 31	F 7 14 21 28	F 4 11 18 25	F 3 10 17 24 31
S 4 11 18 25	S 1 8 15 22 29	S 5 12 19 26	S 4 11 18 25

Stock List. 1977-78

CHASSIS No.	Sold To.	DATE Sold
75116897	John M. Morrison 93 N Tolsta Lewis	26·1·78
9B08DGY 130592	Miss Terri O. Shannon 2 Drinishader Harris	14·10·77
92170GY 705123	Donald John Macleod 1 Seaforst Locks	18·3·77
92170GY 705617	Thomas Tyson North End Carnishader UIG	1·11·77
92170GY 705742	Angus John MacDonald 2 Clevette Locks	19·9·77
92170GY 705854	Donald McDonald 22 Crossbost Locks	7·10·77
9170EGY 611300	Kenneth MacKenzieLtd SeaviewRd SY	23·6·77
9K69DGY 134428	Thomas McBratney 54 Springfield Rd SY	28·3·77
9K69DGY 135780	Peter George Ross 10 Scott Rd TARBERT	10·10·77
9B70CGX 134130	Demo	6·9·77
9170QGY 614131	Joe Black Manor Farm SY	24·8·77
9170 EGY 613827	Donald MacKinlay 30 Coplonway	1·8·77
E1M3BEO-GW-106634	Duncan Thurlow Ltd. Maritime Bldg SY	1·4·77
9B08DGY 138740	Demo	30·4·77
9C69DGX 138717	Harris Tweed Association 6 Seden Rd. SY	21·12·77
7775149401	Mrs Mary Corrigton AM FASGASH' Lease	17·5·77
7675199572	Demo	25·4·77
9B70CGX 134957	Carline MacLeod 10 Peterson Drive SY	4·8·77
" 134788	Demo	9·1·78
9C69DGX 138306	Demo	25·4·78
9B08DGY 154775	Demo	9·1·78
7675218939	Dr Eric Brotheroyd 14 Smithell Cresent SY	16·8·77
9C69DGX 138338	John Murray 30 N Tolsta Lewis	30·6·78
9F64DGX 134336	John MacLean LakeView' Knockaird NESS	26·6·78
9F64DGX 134581	Robert Summerford 49 Parkend Sandwick SY	1·8·77
7675143441	Demo	9·1·78
7675250535	Donald Gunn 1 Port of Ness	11·11·77
9B08DGY 162533	Miss Mary McDonald '51 Swordale Point	4·1·78
7675269188	Demo	9·1·78
9B08DGY 163061	Angus Munroe 93 Newmarket SY	9·1·78
9B08DGY 162713	Steph. J. Maher 5 Crawford way, New Malden Surrey	27·10·78
9B08DGY 162560	Demo	9·1·78
76 HY106860	Demo	9·1·78
HY100221	Peter Cardwell 36 Barony Square SY	29·6·78
7775 049929	John McKenzie 79 Springfield Rd SY	7·3·78
9F70GHY 603972	Joe Black Manor Farm SY	4·1·78
9B70CGX 611376	Transferred to Templeton Bros Edinburgh &c Glasgow	6·2·78
85076830	Donald M Graham 25A Upper Bayble Point	17·5·78
9B15 DHX 117041	Demo	11·5·78
7685127944	Murdo MacRitchie 2 St Ronan's Drive Leonal	2·6·78
76 HY 127642	Douglas Brekke 64 South Beach St. SY	26·4·78

From 1·1·77

NEW VEHICLE

NEW VEHICLE STOCK No.	DATE BOUGHT	VEHICLE TYPE		COLOUR	REG No.
272	20·1·77	Cavalier 'L' 1600 4 Door Saloon		Jade Green Met	MSS 608 S
273	24·1·77	Chevette 'L' Hatchback		Cardinal Red	MSS 166 S
274	26·1·77	Bedford HA 6 cwt Van		Cargo Green	LJS 4 R
275	26·1·77	Bedford HA 6 cwt Van			MSS 169 S
276	26·1·77	Bedford HA 6 cwt Van		Cargo Blue	MSS 166 S
277	26·1·77	Bedford HA 6 cwt Van			LJS 503 R
278	31·1·77	Bedford CF Petrol Van		Cargo Green	LJS 187 R
279	4·2·77	VX 1800 4 Door Saloon		Light Blue Met	LJS 6 R
280	17·2·77	VX 1800 4 Door Saloon		Ruby	MSS 165 S
281	22·2·77	Bedford Chevanne 3 Door Van		Coppertone	MSS 62 S
282	22·2·77	Bedford CF Diesel Van 18 cwt		Cargo Grey	MSS 61 S
283	23·2·77	Petrol		Cargo Orange	LJS 806 S
284 (SAT)	26·2·77	KD/151 D/215 Alloy Petrol Tanker		Dark Green	LJS 7 R
285	1·3·77	Chevette E Hatch 3door		Cardinal Red	LJS 188 R
286	24·3·77	Viva E 4 door Saloon		Estro Light Blue	MSS 296 S
287	25·3·77	Cavalier 1600 4 dr GL (Auto) Saloon	L Auto	Sapphire Blue	LJS 186 R
288	21·4·77			Amber Gold	NJS 177 S
289	5·5·77	CHEVANNE 3 door VAN		Cardinal Red	LJS 862 S
290	3·5·77			Bright Satin Metallic	MSS 603 S
291	25·5·77	Viva E 4 door Saloon		Cardinal Red	MSS 903 S
292	26·5·77	Chevette 'L' HATCH			NJS 404 S
293	26·5·77	Cavalier L 4 door Saloon		Sapphire Blue	LJS 868 S
294	31·5·77	Viva E 4 door Saloon		Cardinal Red	NJS 351 S
295	31·5·77	Viva GLS 4 door Saloon		Light Blue Met	NJS 301 S
296	16·6·77			Bright Satin Met	LJS 864 S
297	24·6·77	Cavalier 'L' 4 door Saloon		Cardinal Red	MSS 606 S
298	28·6·77			Pastel Blue	MSS 195 S
299	7·7·77	Chevette 'L' HATCH		Light Blue Met	OJS 801 T
300	14·7·77	Cavalier L 4 door Saloon		Pastel Beige	MSS 609 S
301	27·7·77	Chevette 'L' HATCH		Ruby	MSS 609 S
302	5·8·77			Lindera Green	OJS 604 T
303	16·8·77			Pastel Beige	MSS 604 S
304	30·9·77	Cavalier 'L' 4 door Saloon (EXT Auto Gear)		Jade Green	MSS 605 S
305	15·11·77	VX 1800 Saloon (Auto)(with S.A.T.)		Ruby	NSS 568 S
306	19·11·77	Cavalier 1900 GL 4 dr		Lindera Green	OJS 611 S
307	1·11·77	Bedford CF 18cwt DIESEL VAN		Cargo Orange	MSS 397 S
308	16·12·77	CHEVANNE		Sapphire Blue	
309	30·12·77	Cavalier 1600 GL 4 door Saloon		Crystal Blue	NJS 347 S
310	26·1·78	Chevette 'L' ESTATE		Jamaica Yellow	PJS 489 T
311	15·2·78	Cavalier 1600 L 4 door Saloon		Ember Red	NJS 462 S
312	17·2·78			Sapphire Blue Met.	NJS 173 S

The big Mack was taken over to Borve on the West side, a digger ripped the cab off it and the engine was put into a fishing vessel. The last one, Ian Mitchell's favourite, was the Bedford that he bought from SMT in Glasgow; he had that one right up until the garage shut and then he donated it to a man in Newmarket – he gave it to him for nothing and it lay outside and just fell to bits – the grill part and the original number plate are hanging on my garage wall. The only two parts left plus the registration documents.

I remember the big Mack getting called out one time in the winter time   an aeroplane at the airport was coming in to land and when it came to the end it went into ice and slid off the runway. Ian Mitchell and Norman went down to see if they could get it back onto the hard, the tarmac, without damaging it, that plane weighed 32 tons and they were shown where to put the ropes for towing so they wouldn't damage it, and Norman went into the cab, put it into first gear, no throttle, nothing, just on idle, pulled it back on. Straight back on, absolutely no damage.

The same lorry was sent over to Uig; something happened, there was air brakes on that lorry and there was no back up at all so they lost the air brake. It went off the road and practically buried itself into the peat – they had to get a digger to make a road behind it, hitched the cables, it was hydraulics that was on that thing and pulled itself back out onto the road, probably with a wee bit of assistance from other lorries. They came back into the garage, cab repaired, back on the road again.

The trucks would always be sitting where the roundabout is today, in line across the road. He was really into tow wagons, he had leaflets and pictures of ones he was going to buy.

Opposite: Examples of Ian's meticulous record keeping.
New car sales, a vehicle stock list, and second-hand cars.

23. THE END OF AN ERA

Ian Mitchell retired in 1995. After forty-four years involved in the business and at the age of sixty-two, he closed the garage and terminated the Vauxhall dealership. Ian's son Christopher had not shared his father's interests in the motor trade, and had not entered into the family business. This was the end of an era, and it was some time before the people of Stornoway could accept that there was no Mitchell's Garage.

It had not been a sudden decision to end the business, and Ian Mitchell had been seriously assessing the garage operations from the mid-1980s onwards, particularly as some activities were not prospering as they had once done, and financial results were variable; a reasonable profit made in 1987 turned into a small operating loss the following year. It perhaps shows Ian Mitchell's wisdom and foresight that as he grew nearer to retiring age that he realised the time was right to dispose of the business.

In June 1989, Ian Mitchell had the whole business and properties valued. In the valuation, the garage was described as consisting of four buildings, which covered most of the site. These were the original Workshop built around 1946/47, the Showroom constructed in 1969/70, the Parts Department situated to the rear which had been added in the early 1970s, and the newest part, the Office Block, which had been built to the front in 1974/75. All the buildings were in an adequate condition. In the Workshop there were three vehicle ramps, a Rolling Road MOT Tester, a fully equipped Body Shop and a Compressor. Outside was a Pump Island, contained beneath a somewhat old-fashioned canopy in front of the Office Block. The island had three pumps, selling four star and unleaded petrol, and diesel. A small Petrol Sales Kiosk formed part of the Office building. There were three 3,000 gallon underground petrol storage tanks.

The garage in 1995, prior to being sold.

Ian checks the petrol storage tanks. Even after he had ceased to sell petrol, the storage tanks had to be regularly checked to measure any water which might have seeped into them.

In addition to the garage premises John Mitchell (Stornoway) Ltd owned a dwelling house and a dwelling house and shop. The former, at 46 Bayhead Street, was a single storey and attic stone-built house and was in reasonable condition. The other property, 44/45 Bayhead Street, was a two storey structure; it had been unoccupied for some time and was suffering from damp, another casualty of the flooding in the area. These properties were sold by the company in the late 1980s.

Sales of petrol were declining, from 63,315 gallons in 1986 to 53,035 gallons in 1988. In the light of this Ian Mitchell took the decision in August 1990 to end the sale of fuel and not to renew his licence for selling petrol. The petrol pumps were duly removed from the forecourt, but dealing with the storage tanks was a much more demanding operation. In a letter from the Senior Trading Standards Officer of the Western Isles, Ian was informed that, 'petrol storage tanks represent a major hazard and must be rendered safe as soon as possible. To do this the tanks should first be gas-freed and then filled in solid with cement slurry. The person carrying out the gas-freeing of the tanks should advise this department [Trading Standards] of the method he proposes to use, and at the end of the operation should provide us with a suitable certificate.' It was certainly not just a case of emptying the tanks and closing the manhole covers. The task would not be completed for four years.

In 1991 Ian Mitchell obtained a former BP tanker lorry and at various times used it to check the contents of all three tanks. Records show that the leaded petrol tank, nearest to Bayhead Street, was 'full of water and the dipstick felt like it was going thru' sand and gravel, at the bottom of the tank.' When Ian tested the contents of the central tank in 1992 the dipstick showed that there was about 800 gallons of water, almost a quarter of the tank's capacity. By 1993 this had increased to over 1,000 gallons, and just before the tank was finally sealed off it contained about 1,300 gallons of water. The effect of the underground drainage and tides was still being felt. Finally, in August 1994, Ian reported that, 'the covers and frames [had been] removed, both manholes filled in with gravel and cemented over.' He could now inform the Trading Standards Officer that the task had been completed.

Perhaps indicative of the impending decline of the business, the roof of the showroom was removed, leaving gleaming new cars exposed to the elements. It was, however, a cost saving action, as the company was no longer required to pay business rates on that section of the garage.

The financial implications of selling the business were carefully considered by Ian Mitchell and the decision to sell was reached. The properties and business were duly advertised for sale. Ian's preference was for a share sale, retaining ownership of the land and buildings and leasing them to an interested company. Interest was shown by Mackays Garage and Agricultural Co Ltd, who owned a Vauxhall franchised garage in Dingwall. After due consideration, they withdrew their interest, as they felt that the premises too large, while Ian's preferred share transfer would incur too many complications.

In 1995 D R Macleod, owner of the local haulage company D R Macleod Ltd, entered into an agreement to purchase the entire shareholding of John Mitchell (Stornoway) Ltd. D R's intention, as he wrote in a letter to Vauxhall Motors Ltd, was to 'continue to operate the business as before, i.e. from the same dealership premises, with the same trained and experienced staff, engaged in new and used vehicle sales, aftersales, M.O.T. testing, Body and paint and self-drive hire, using exclusively the Vauxhall car range.' This agreement eventually fell through.

In May 1995, with no other prospects for selling the garage business in sight, Ian Mitchell relinquished his Vauxhall Franchise and made plans to close operations. A farewell dinner was held by Vauxhall, after which the Vauxhall dealer Planning Director, M J Tearle, commented, 'You have certainly added a great deal of value to all of us that have

Ian in retirement – hill-walking.

been fortunate to know you in bringing a touch of the island life into our hectic world, and with such good humour too!'

Finally, in 1996, the property was sold to Norman L Macdonald, who was eventually to reopen the site as a filling station and shop. It was to be known as Manor Filling Station, replacing a petrol station of that name located slightly further out of the town. The name of Mitchell would no longer be seen at the corner of Matheson Road and Bayhead Street.

At the time of the closure the garage had employed a staff of thirteen. In the Workshop there were two mechanics, a body repairer and a receptionist. There were two office staff and one each dealt with the Parts Department, Car Sales and Car Hire respectively. There was a part time cleaner. In addition, three part time employees had dealt with Petrol Sales until these ended in 1990. Some of the staff had worked for the Mitchells for many years and their length of service was duly rewarded. Ina Matheson, who had started working in Mitchell's Garage office when she was sixteen, and Norman Macleod both had over twenty years' service and Joan Macleod had worked for Mitchell's for twelve years.

Ian in retirement – relaxing.

Life in retirement for Ian Mitchell

Ian had always kept busy outside work, particularly as an active member of the Stornoway Rotary Club, becoming President, and holding other offices in the Club. He was a founder member and Past President of the Stornoway Chamber of Commerce, and was a member of the Stornoway Speaker's Club in the 1970s. He was a keen oenologist, and his choice of wine when dining out always reflected his knowledge in this field. Other interests included hill walking in Lewis, Harris and further afield, including the West Highland Way; travelling internationally with his sister in the 1980s and 90s, and later on to Formula One Grand Prix with friends; astrology; and classic country music – for a short time in his retirement he organized and ran a country music club, the Cottonwood Club.

Ian's wife Anne unexpectedly passed away in 1998; this had a significant impact on Ian, and many felt it took him years to process his loss. That said, during retirement Ian certainly did not become inactive. He was a man of many varied interests and tastes. He continued his love of and interest in cars by founding the Western Isles Classic Car Club — he was often seen driving through Stornoway and further afield in his classic Vauxhall cars. He also co-founded the Stornoway Currency Club, for amateur stock investors (Ian was dedicated to the investment principles of Warren Buffett, the

Ian Mitchell, President of the Rotary Club of Stornoway, 1980-81.

successful American investor and philanthropist), he used his business acumen as a Business Counsellor with Western Isles Enterprise, and developed his interest in the history of Lewis through identifying and marking historic sites. This included commissioning a handsome monument to the Seaforth Highlanders located at the head of Loch Seaforth, on the site of the old castle of the Mackenzies of Seaforth, and the stone 'teardrop' at Airidhbhruaich which Ian commissioned to commemorate the landing on Lewis of Prince Charles Edward Stuart when fleeing the aftermath of the Battle of Culloden. This was described as 'the political even handedness of Ian's philanthropy.'

As the years went by Ian Mitchell did suffer some health problems. In 2007, he successfully underwent a heart bypass operation, from which he gained a further lease of life. During the following decade, while he physically slowed down, he remained as mentally alert and active as ever. It was therefore a shock when the news appeared that Ian Mitchell had passed away in his own home on the morning of 29 December 2016, a few weeks after his eighty-third birthday.

Only three years before he died, in December 2013, Ian Mitchell had organised an eightieth birthday party at the Caladh Inn in Stornoway; among the large number who were invited were many of his former employees. It is a fitting tribute to him that over sixty retired garage staff, bus drivers and conductresses attended the event, with many treating the occasion as a Mitchell's reunion as much as a birthday party. Ian realised afterwards that he'd missed a few former employees from his invitation list, and made sure he treated them to a separate meal! It all says more than words can do about the esteem with which he was held.

WESTERN LEWIS COACHES LTD.

REGISTERED OFFICE

JOHN MITCHELL (STORNOWAY) LTD.

REGISTERED OFFICE

It is the aim of this dealership to provide the best possible service for each and every one of our customers.

Your satisfaction is our main concern.

If you have any comments to make regarding the service you receive from this department, please contact me personally.

SAD 529

TITLE J M Mitchell